בס"ד

Annual Testimonial Dinner

of

Congregation Beth Sholom

Lawrence, New York

In honor of
Rabbi Joseph Glatzer

April 1, 1990
6 Nisan 5750

מסורה

ArtScroll Mesorah Series®

Expositions on Jewish liturgy and thought

Rabbi Nosson Scherman / Rabbi Meir Zlotowitz

General Editors

אגרת הרמב"ן

A Letter
for the Ages

A Letter

by
Rabbi Avrohom Chaim Feuer

אגרת הרמב"ן

for the Ages

IGGERES HARAMBAN / *The Ramban's ethical letter with an anthology of contemporary Rabbinic expositions.*

Published by

Mesorah Publications, ltd

FIRST EDITION
First Impression . . . September, 1989

Published and Distributed by
MESORAH PUBLICATIONS, Ltd.
Brooklyn, New York 11232

Distributed in Israel by
MESORAH MAFITZIM / J. GROSSMAN
Rechov Harav Uziel 117
Jerusalem, Israel

Distributed in Europe by
J. LEHMANN HEBREW BOOKSELLERS
20 Cambridge Terrace
Gateshead, Tyne and Wear
England NE8 1RP

Distributed in Australia & New Zealand by
GOLD'S BOOK & GIFT CO.
36 William Street
Balaclava 3183, Vic., Australia

Distributed in South Africa by
KOLLEL BOOKSHOP
22 Muller Street
Yeoville 2198, South Africa

ARTSCROLL MESORAH SERIES®
"IGGERES HARAMBAN" / A Letter for the Ages
© Copyright 1989, by MESORAH PUBLICATIONS, Ltd.
4401 Second Avenue / Brooklyn, N.Y. 11232 / (718) 921-9000

ISBN
0-89906-218-0 (hard cover)
0-89906-219-9 (paperback)

Typography by Compuscribe at ArtScroll Studios, Ltd.

Printed in the United States of America by Noble Book Press
Bound by Sefercraft, Quality Bookbinders, Ltd. Brooklyn, N.Y.

לעלוי נשמת הרה"ח

ר' נחום יואל הלפרן

בהרה"ח **חיים יעקב** זצ"ל

אהובם ואיש אימונם של גדולי הדור

הפליג בפעולות וחיזוק התורה, הדת והחסד

ולא מחזיק טיבותא לנפשיה

נלב"ע בשם טוב

ה' כסלו תשמ"ז

∼§ Preface

Hashem granted me the privilege of studying Torah for many years in the Telshe Yeshiva of Cleveland. Throughout my years there I noticed that my *Rabbeim* and friends had a very special feeling for the *Iggeres HaRamban*. Often at the conclusion of the weekday *davening* I would hear someone chanting this letter slowly, deliberately, with deep emotion — word by word — line by line; spirit soaring and lips aflame with fervor. These images left a profound impression on me.

Since then, I have reviewed this letter hundreds of times, and it never fails to fascinate me anew each time I read it. Effortlessly it succeeds in conveying the essential teaching of *mussar* and self-improvement in a few pithy paragraphs. Indeed, every review produces fresh insight and a reinforced commitment to practice the ideals which *Ramban* teaches.

Over the years I have discovered the power of this letter. *Ramban* promises that "every day that you shall read this letter, heaven shall answer your heart's desires." Indeed, as one internalizes its lessons, he grows spiritually. As his character grows, so his fortunes change. Thus, some have the custom of reciting it when they face difficulty or danger. A bride and groom, standing at the gates of their new life, recite the letter on their wedding day. Likewise, there is a custom in some *kehillos* to publicly recite the letter (or portions of it) before the sounding of the *shofar* on *Rosh Hashanah*. Indeed, the Talmud (*Rosh*

Hashanah 26b) teaches that the shape of a *shofar* resembles a man bent over humbly in intense prayer. *Ramban's* letter, with his profound emphasis on the quality of humility, sets a fitting mood for supplication on the Day of Judgment.

For all its philosophical richness, *Ramban's* letter is first and foremost a work of *mussar*: a practical treatise of ethics that hopes to touch the lives of its readers. When studying it, one must not read with his eyes alone — he must open his heart as well. Thus, as with all works of *mussar*, הִתְבּוֹנְנוּת (contemplation) is crucial. *Ramban's* letter is concise as well as subtle. In the book that follows, I have attempted to elaborate on the *Ramban's* themes at length, and to illustrate them with anecdotes. The text divides the letter into thirty sections, each one highlighting and expanding upon one of the essential concepts taught in this letter. It is suggested that the reader peruse only one section at a time, every day of the month, thereby allowing time for adequate meditation and internalization of each concept.

It is my fervent hope that the reader will be inspired by this letter and merit *Ramban's* blessing that "every day that you shall read this letter, heaven shall answer your heart's desires."

❦   ❦   ❦

I take this opportunity to express my deep appreciation to Congregation Ohr Chaim, whom I am privileged to serve as Rav. This work would have been impossible without the members of the *kehillah*, who constantly encourage me to study Torah and to write. I thank them for sharing with me ten wonderful years of growth in Torah and *yiras shamayim*.

My *chaveirim*, **Rabbi Meir Zlotowitz** and **Rabbi Nosson Scherman**, saw the merit in the concept of this work and have turned it into a fully developed volume. It has been my great privilege to work with them on various volumes of the ArtScroll Series over the past thirteen years and I rejoice over their success and *siyata dishmaya*.

As always, **Rabbi Sheah Brander's** artistic skills have made this volume a thing of beauty — a delight for the eye and the mind.

Rabbi Avie Gold served as project director for this volume and his expertise, friendship and good nature make it a pleasure to work with him.

Rabbi Yehezkel Danziger has taken time from his own busy schedule to help supervise the editing process.

Rabbi David Fohrman skillfully edited this work and used his special feel for words and concepts to polish every phrase and thought. Rabbi Fohrman's talents have immensely enhanced this work and the finished product is a tribute to his knowledge and pen.

Rabbi Elchonon Yosef Hertzman is a lifelong friend. His guidance and encouragement have assisted the preparation of this work.

I am grateful to those who participated in the typing and proof-reading: **Mrs. Faygie Weinbaum, Mrs. Menucha Silver, Mrs. Zissi Landau** and **Bassie Goldstein**.

The entire Mesorah Publications' staff helps make it possible for such works to be produced and disseminated: **Rabbi Shimon Golding, Rabbi Yosef Gesser, Yosef Timinsky, Lea Freier, Sheila Tennenbaum, Mrs. Surie Maline** and **Faigie Zlotowitz**.

Shmuel Blitz, director of ArtScroll/Jerusalem, remains a vital member of the team that has made a monumental contribution to Torah knowledge in our generation.

My father-in-law, **HaGaon HaRav Mordechai Gifter**, שליט״א, the *Rosh Yeshivah* of Telshe, is one of the precious resources of our generation, but as the crown and guide of our family, he is even more to us. As rebbi, guide, father, and inspiration, his presence hovers over every word of this volume.

ArtScroll's *Reb Moshe* by Rabbi Shimon Finkelman served as the source for many of the illustrative anecdotes included in this work. Some anecdotes were culled from Rav Chaim Ephraim Zeitchik's classic *Meoros Hagedolim*, and its English version, *Sparks of Mussar*.

Last to be mentioned, yet foremost in mind, is my wife Luba Rochel, מנב״ת. Her enthusiasm for this project always inspired me and made every moment of work a pleasure.

Today we are celebrating the *bar mitzvah* of our son Shmuel Zalman, נ״י, and we pray that *Hashem* will grant us much Torah *nachas* from him and his brothers Tzvi, Eliyahu Meir, Simcha Yeshaya and Eliezer, נ״י. May they be guided by the opening words of *Ramban's* letter, which quotes the wisdom of Shlomo HaMelech: *Heed my son the discipline of your father and do not forsake the guidance of your mother (Proverbs 1:8).*

Finally, my inexpressible gratitude to *Hashem Yisborach* for His blessings and for permitting me to help spread His word.

Avrohom Chaim Feuer

Miami Beach, Florida
14 Av 5749 / August 15, 1989

לזכר נשמת דודי היקר
ר׳ שלמה הרשל בן ר׳ יוסף אליעזר ע״ה
נפטר לעולמו י״ד כסלו תשמ״ט

In memory of our beloved uncle
Mr Harry Levitz, of blessed memory,
whose ways were always soft and gentle
and whose days were filled with
kindness and compassion.

14 Kislev 5749 — Nov. 22, 1988

ᷓ§ Introduction

The Letter of Ramban, also known as *Iggeres HaMussar*, occupies a special place in the world of Torah literature. This epistle has been reprinted countless times — on its own, and in *siddurim*, *machzorim*, *Tehillim* and *mussar* anthologies. It is recited and studied regularly by masses of Jews who hold dear the lessons of this letter and try to live in accordance with its lofty spirit. Through the ages, Ramban's letter has been cherished by Torah scholars as well as the masses of Jewry.

The following remarks come from the ethical work *Meulefes Sappirim* and they are printed as a preface to many published editions of *Ramban's* letter:

> This letter was sent by *Ramban* from the city of Acre in *Eretz Yisrael* to his son, Nachman, in Catalina, Spain, to inspire him to act with humility. He instructed his son to read this letter once every week and to teach it to his children as well, so that they might learn it by heart, in order to train them in their youth to fear God.

> *Ramban* assured his son that on the day that he read this letter his wishes would be fulfilled from heaven. Also, *Ramban* promised that whomever would accustom himself to read this letter would be spared of tribulation, and would become worthy of the life of the World to Come.

Similarly, the *Chida* (acronym for Rav Chaim Yoseif David Azulai) writes in his *Shem HaGedolim*:

> In this letter to his son Nachman, *Ramban* outlines a program for achieving the qualities of sanctity and humility, and makes a pledge that on the day that one reads this letter, heaven will answer the reader's requests. The חַכְמֵי הַמּוּסָר, *masters of mussar*

encouraged their students to study this letter periodically, for *Ramban's* holy words have the power to penetrate the innermost recesses of the heart, permeating it with a spirit of sanctity. The message of the letter will make the reader profoundly aware of God's Omnipresence and his own relative frailty . . . Fortunate is the person who listens to *Ramban's* words, he will achieve serenity and peace of mind.

⋈§ Sparks of Fire

Rabbi Moshe ben Nachman, more widely referred to by his acronym *Ramban*, and known in English as Nachmanides, was born in Gerona, in northern Spain in the year 4955 (1195) to a prominent Rabbinical family. He studied under Rabbi Yehudah ben Yakar and Rabbi Nosson ben Meir of Trinquetaille, and eventually became recognized as the foremost halachic authority in Spain. As his stature grew, his rulings became highly respected in other countries as well. Indeed, a century after *Ramban* passed on, the great Spanish rav, Rabbi Yitzchak ben Sheshes Perfet [known as *"Rivash"* (1326-1407)] writes of him: "All his words are like sparks of fire, and entire communities of Castille rely upon his halachic ruling as if given directly from the Almighty to Moses."

Ramban was an extremely prolific writer and he authored classic works on all areas of Torah. He is best known for his novellae (*chiddushim*) on most of the Talmud in the style of the French Tosafists and his monumental commentary on the Torah. The latter work is unique in that it not only interprets verses, but also analyzes major themes of Jewish thought and fundamentals of our faith.

In 1263, *Ramban* was ordered by King James of Aragon to hold a religious disputation with a Jewish apostate, Pablo Christiani, at Barcelona. The king and his court, including many dignitaries of the church, were present at this dispute. Although *Ramban* was not allowed to explicitly take the offensive, he succeeded in his defense of Judaism to discredit all Christian claims of authenticity based upon the Bible or Talmud. Later, he published a verbatim account of the debate under the title *Sefer HaVikuach*. The priests of the Dominican order claimed that many passages in this work were blasphemous attacks against Christianity and thus had the *Sefer HaVikuach* condemned to be burned. As a consequence, *Ramban* was expelled from the kingdom of Aragon.

At the age of seventy-two, *Ramban* settled in *Eretz Yisrael*. After a difficult journey, he arrived in the port of Acco [Acre] in the month of Elul, 1267. According to the tradition cited by *Meulefes Sappirim* (quoted above) it was at this time that *Ramban* wrote his *Iggeres HaMussar* to his son Nachman in Spain. In the Holy Land, *Ramban* truly felt that he stood in God's immediate Presence; one can sense his ecstasy in this short letter which is suffused with love and fear of God.

During his first Elul in Israel, *Ramban* traveled to Jerusalem to spend *Rosh Hashanah* there. What he found was a city of ruins, plundered by the brutal conquest of the Crusaders. In another famous letter to his son Nachman, *Ramban* describes the situation:

> And what shall I tell you in regard to this land? Many are its forsaken places and great are its wasted areas. The truth of the matter is: The more sacred the place, the greater the devastation it has suffered. Jerusalem is the most desolate place of all. . .

In his letter, *Ramban* describes how he designated an abandoned house as a synagogue and brought a Torah scroll from the city of Shechem. On *Rosh Hashanah*, *Ramban* delivered a sermon there, and exhorted the few Jews who remained in *Eretz Yisrael* to be exceedingly careful that their actions be righteous; for they are like servants in the king's palace who must continually be aware of their master's presence.

For more than three centuries, *Ramban's* synagogue was a beloved landmark for Jewish pilgrims who made the arduous trip to visit Jerusalem. However, sometime in the sixteenth century the Moslem government confiscated the holy structure and turned it into a mosque. When the Old City of Jerusalem was liberated in 1967, this site was in ruins. It has since been restored to its former beauty and serves as a vibrant synagogue and *beis midrash* today. The words of this *Iggeres* are inscribed in bold letters on the walls of its renovated sanctuary.

After his visit to Jerusalem, *Ramban* settled in Acre, a Torah center of the time, and taught a group of devoted disciples. He died there in the year 1270 (11 Nissan 5030). Various historians place *Ramban's* burial site at Hebron, near the cave of Machpelah, Haifa, Acco or in Jerusalem.

The history work, *Shalsheles HaKabbalah* (by Gedaliah ibn Yachya, 1515-1587), relates a fascinating tradition concerning *Ramban's* death. When *Ramban* departed from Spain to far-off *Eretz Yisrael*, his disciples asked him how they would know the day of his demise. *Ramban* replied: "On the day of my death a crack will appear in the tombstone on the grave of my mother, of blessed memory. This will be the sign that I have passed away."

Some four years after Ramban's departure, one of his student's found that the gravestone had cracked. Thereupon, the entire House of Israel became aware of their tremendous loss and mourned for their beloved teacher.

⊷§ Two Versions

The *Iggeres HaRamban* was printed for the first time in Mantua, Italy, in 1623 as part of the *sefer Tapuchei Zahav* by Rabbi Yechiel Mili. It was later printed in the classic *mussar* work *Reishis Chachmah* by Eliyahu de Vidas (a disciple of the Kabbalist, Rabbi Moshe Cordovero) in his essay on humility entitled *Shaar HaAnavah* (ch. 6).

The text which appears in those books has since been accepted as the authentic version of the letter. This volume is based on this original version. However, various anthologies cite a second, expanded version of the letter which essentially parallels the first, with minor additions. The reader is referred to Rabbi Chaim Dov Chavel's work, *Kol Kisvei HaRamban* Vol. I, for the entire text of the second version and a critical comparison of the two version of the letter.[1]

⊷§ Ethical Refinement: A Foundation of Ramban's Philosophy

The concept of *mussar*, self-discipline, occupies an important place in *Ramban's* thinking, teaching and writing. Generally, the term *mussar* refers to the pursuit of self-control, the perfection of one's character, and the purification of one's motives and values. These are the lofty themes which *Ramban* addresses frequently in his works, and especially in this *Iggeres*.

Ramban's philosophy of Judaism is complex and cannot be adequately portrayed in a few short lines. Nevertheless, a theme which penetrates much of his thought is: לֹא נִתְּנוּ הַמִּצְוֹת אֶלָּא לְצָרֵף אֶת הַבְּרִיּוֹת, *The sole purpose of God's mitzvos is to refine and purify mankind* (see

---

1. This year (5749/1989) a new commentary on *Iggeres HaRamban* was published. It was authored by Rabbi Chaim Aryeh Erlanger and it is also based on the first, original version of this letter. Some of the sources cited in Rabbi Erlanger's work are quoted in this volume.

his commentary to *Deut*. 22:1). Just as the crucible separates the dross from precious metals, so do the *mitzvos* expel the impurities from the hearts of men. Man's nature, if left unbridled, can become harsh and coarse; therefore, the Almighty designed *mitzvos* which would accustom the heart to compassion and sensitivity. Thus, according to *Ramban*, God insists that we display kindness towards animals, not so much because of His concern for these creatures, but because of His concern for *us*. If we act unkindly towards a feeling, living creature, we implant a streak of cruelty within ourselves. God, however, desires that we sculpt our personalities to imitate His perfect ways: Just as the Almighty is caring, merciful and compassionate, so must we be (see *Talmud, Shabbos* 133b). *Ramban* views in a similar manner: One is affected spiritually and physically by what one eats . The flesh of a wild beast, a predator, can have a powerful and detrimental affect upon the character of the one who eats it.

In a similar vein, *Ramban* writes that the *mitzvos* which command us to remember God's miracles are not designed for God's sake, but for our own. By acknowledging God's wondrous kindness and salvation our hearts are imbued with the positive traits of gratitude and humility and our souls are suffused with love of God. Every *mitzvah* improves man. Each addresses itself to another *middah* — character trait — so that ultimately the person who fulfills *all* of God's *mitzvos* will become a paragon of virtue.

Ramban's emphasis on ethical refinement has indeed been shared by the sages of all generations. King Solomon said: הַחֲזֵק בַּמּוּסָר אַל תֶּרֶף נִצְּרֶהָ כִּי הִיא חַיֶּיךָ, *Cling tightly to ethical discipline, do not let loose! Guard it carefully, for it is your life* (Proverbs 4:13). The *Vilna Gaon* comments that man was created so that he may eliminate his negative character traits. The person who fails to accomplish this has lived to no avail. Similarly, *Rambam* (Maimonides) writes in his introduction to *Avos* (*Shemonah Perakim LeHaRambam*, ch. 4): הָאָדָם הַשָּׁלֵם צָרִיךְ לוֹ שֶׁיִּזְכּוֹר מְדוֹתָיו תָּמִיד וְיִשְׁקוֹל פְּעוּלוֹתָיו וְיִבְחֹן תְּכוּנוֹת נַפְשׁוֹ יוֹם יוֹם . . . , *The person who strives for perfection must be ever mindful of his middos and he should evaluate his actions and carefully examine his character traits every day . . .*

Finally, *Rabbi Chaim Vital*, the most illustrious disciple of the *Arizal*, writes that the reason there is no direct Torah command to perfect our character is because the observance of the entire Torah is contingent upon it: "A good character is the primary requisite to fulfilling the 613 *mitzvos* . . . Therefore manifesting a faulty character is much more serious than transgressing a command . . . One must be more heedful of evil emotions than of observing the positive and negative commands."

Rav Eliyahu Lopian would illustrate *Rav Chaim Vital's* statement with a parable: Once a builder signed a contract obligating himself to build a structure for a certain fixed price. Upon completion of the building, the builder was paid the stipulated sum, yet the builder wanted more. "You must pay me extra for the excavation and laying of the foundation!" argued the builder.

The landlord, however, adamantly refused to pay. "When I contracted for the whole structure, the foundation was certainly included. Can you imagine a building without a foundation? With no solid base a structure is worthless, and will surely collapse."

Similarly, said *Rav Eliyahu Lopian*, God commanded Israel to structure themselves according to a Divine blueprint. But to accomplish this, they must perfect their character traits, for good character is the foundation of the human structure. A person must dig deep into the soil of his heart and lay a foundation of sensitivity, humility, and fear of God. Only on such a solid base can he build his personal edifice.

Ramban compiled this *Iggeres* to aid his son in laying the foundations of his own spiritual structure. Since its first appearance centuries ago, it has been a classic work of inspiration, guiding the lives of generations. It is my hope that the reader of this volume and its collected comments will find himself stirred by the powerful yet personal messages that reverberate in major chords through the soul of *Ramban's* timeless words.

אגרת הרמב"ן

A Letter
for the Ages

The Ramban's Letter

Heed, my son, the discipline of your father, and do not
forsake the guidance of your mother.[1] Accustom
yourself to speak gently to all people at all times. This
will protect you from anger — a most serious character
flaw which causes one to sin. Our Rabbis taught:[2]
"Whoever flares up in anger is subject to the discipline
of Gehinnom, as it is written: Banish anger from your
heart and remove evil from your flesh.[3] The evil
mentioned here refers to Gehinnom, as it is written:
And the wicked are destined for the day of evil."[4]

Once you have distanced yourself from anger, the
quality of humility will enter your heart. This sterling
quality is the finest of all admirable traits, as Scripture
writes: On the heels of humility comes the fear of
HASHEM.[5] Through humility, the fear of God will
intensify in your heart, for you will always be aware of
from where you have come and to where you are
destined to go. You will realize that in life you are as frail
as the maggot or the worm — all the more so in death. It
is this sense of humility which reminds you of the One
before Whom you will be called for judgment — the King
of Glory. Of Him it is written: Behold, heaven and the
heaven of heavens cannot contain You,[6] surely not the
hearts of men.[7] Furthermore, it is written: Do I not fill
heaven and earth? says HASHEM.[8]

After you give serious thought to these ideas you will
stand in awe of your Creator and will be guarded against
sin. Once you have acquired these fine qualities, you will
indeed be happy with your lot.

When your actions display genuine humility — when
you stand meekly before man, and fearfully before
God; when you stand wary of sin — then the spirit

---

(1) *Proverbs* 1:8. (2) *Nedarim* 22a. (3) *Ecclesiastes* 11:10. (4) *Proverbs* 16:4. (5) *Proverbs* 22:4.
(6) *I Kings* 8:27; *II Chronicles* 6:18. (7) *Proverbs* 15:11. (8) *Jeremiah* 23:24.

אִגֶּרֶת הָרַמְבַּ"ן

שְׁמַע בְּנִי מוּסַר אָבִיךָ, וְאַל תִּטֹּשׁ תּוֹרַת אִמֶּךָ.[1] תִּתְנַהֵג תָּמִיד לְדַבֵּר כָּל דְּבָרֶיךָ בְּנַחַת לְכָל אָדָם וּבְכָל עֵת, וּבָזֶה תִּנָּצֵל מִן הַכַּעַס, שֶׁהִיא מִדָּה רָעָה לְהַחֲטִיא בְּנֵי אָדָם. וְכֵן אָמְרוּ רַבּוֹתֵינוּ ז"ל,[2] כָּל הַכּוֹעֵס כָּל מִינֵי גֵּיהִנָּם שׁוֹלְטִין בּוֹ, שֶׁנֶּאֱמַר: הָסֵר כַּעַס מִלִּבֶּךָ, וְהַעֲבֵר רָעָה מִבְּשָׂרֶךָ,[3] וְאֵין רָעָה אֶלָּא גֵּיהִנָּם, שֶׁנֶּאֱמַר: וְגַם רָשָׁע לְיוֹם רָעָה.[4] וְכַאֲשֶׁר תִּנָּצֵל מִן הַכַּעַס תַּעֲלֶה עַל לִבְּךָ מִדַּת הָעֲנָוָה שֶׁהִיא מִדָּה טוֹבָה מִכָּל הַמִּדּוֹת טוֹבוֹת, שֶׁנֶּאֱמַר: עֵקֶב עֲנָוָה יִרְאַת ה'.[5] וּבַעֲבוּר הָעֲנָוָה תַּעֲלֶה עַל לִבְּךָ מִדַּת הַיִּרְאָה, כִּי תִתֵּן אֶל לִבְּךָ תָּמִיד, מֵאַיִן בָּאתָ, וּלְאָן אַתָּה הוֹלֵךְ, וְשֶׁאַתָּה רִמָּה וְתוֹלֵעָה בְּחַיֶּיךָ, וְאַף כִּי בְּמוֹתָךָ, וְלִפְנֵי מִי אַתָּה עָתִיד לִתֵּן דִּין וְחֶשְׁבּוֹן, לִפְנֵי מֶלֶךְ הַכָּבוֹד, שֶׁנֶּאֱמַר: הִנֵּה הַשָּׁמַיִם וּשְׁמֵי הַשָּׁמַיִם לֹא יְכַלְכְּלוּךָ,[6] אַף כִּי לִבּוֹת בְּנֵי אָדָם,[7] וְנֶאֱמַר: הֲלֹא אֶת־הַשָּׁמַיִם וְאֶת־הָאָרֶץ אֲנִי מָלֵא נְאֻם ה'.[8] וְכַאֲשֶׁר תַּחְשֹׁב אֶת כָּל אֵלֶּה, תִּירָא מִבּוֹרַאֲךָ וְתִשָּׁמֵר מִן הַחֵטְא, וּבַמִּדּוֹת הָאֵלֶּה תִּהְיֶה שָׂמֵחַ בְּחֶלְקֶךָ, וְכַאֲשֶׁר תִּתְנַהֵג בְּמִדַּת הָעֲנָוָה לְהִתְבּוֹשֵׁשׁ מִכָּל אָדָם וּלְהִתְפַּחֵד מִמֶּנּוּ וּמִן הַחֵטְא, אָז תִּשְׁרֶה עָלֶיךָ רוּחַ

of God's Presence will rest upon you, as will the splendor of His Glory; you will live the life of the World to Come.

And now my son, understand clearly that one who is prideful in his heart towards other men rebels against the sovereignty of heaven, for he glorifies himself in God's own robes, for it is written, HASHEM reigns, He dons the mantle of grandeur.[1]

For indeed, of what should man be prideful? If he has wealth — it is Hashem who makes one prosperous. And if honor — does honor not belong to God? As it is written: Wealth and honor come from You[2] — how can one glorify himself with the honor of his Maker? If he takes pride in wisdom — let him understand that God may remove the speech of the most competent and take away the wisdom of the aged.[3]

Thus, all men stand as equals before their Creator. In His fury He casts down the lofty; in His goodwill He elevates the downtrodden. Therefore, humble yourself, for Hashem will lift you.

Thus, I shall explain to you how you may accustom yourself to the quality of humility, to walk with it always.

Let your words be spoken gently;
let your head be bowed.

Cast your eyes downward, and your heart heavenward; and when speaking, do not stare at your listener. Let all men seem greater than you in your eyes: If another is more wise or wealthy than yourself, you must show him respect. And if he is poor, and you are richer or wiser than he, consider that he may be more righteous than yourself: If he sins it is the result of error, while your transgression is deliberate.

In all your words, actions and thoughts — at all times — imagine in your heart that you are standing in the presence of the Holy One, Blessed is He, and

הַשְּׁכִינָה, וְזִיו כְּבוֹדָהּ, וְחַיֵּי עוֹלָם הַבָּא. וְעַתָּה בְּנִי דַּע
וּרְאֵה, כִּי הַמִּתְגָּאֶה בְּלִבּוֹ עַל הַבְּרִיּוֹת, מוֹרֵד הוּא
בְּמַלְכוּת שָׁמַיִם, כִּי מִתְפָּאֵר הוּא בִּלְבוּשׁ מַלְכוּת
שָׁמַיִם, שֶׁנֶּאֱמַר: ה' מָלָךְ גֵּאוּת לָבֵשׁ וְגוֹ'.[1] וּבַמֶּה
יִתְגָּאֶה לֵב הָאָדָם, אִם בְּעֹשֶׁר, ה' מוֹרִישׁ וּמַעֲשִׁיר.
וְאִם בְּכָבוֹד, הֲלֹא לֵאלֹקִים הוּא, שֶׁנֶּאֱמַר: וְהָעֹשֶׁר
וְהַכָּבוֹד מִלְּפָנֶיךָ,[2] וְאֵיךְ מִתְפָּאֵר בִּכְבוֹד קוֹנוֹ. וְאִם
מִתְפָּאֵר בְּחָכְמָה, מֵסִיר שָׂפָה לְנֶאֱמָנִים, וְטַעַם זְקֵנִים
יִקָּח.[3] נִמְצָא הַכֹּל שָׁוֶה לִפְנֵי הַמָּקוֹם, כִּי בְאַפּוֹ מַשְׁפִּיל
גֵּאִים, וּבִרְצוֹנוֹ מַגְבִּיהַּ שְׁפָלִים, לָכֵן הַשְׁפִּיל עַצְמְךָ
וִינַשְּׂאֲךָ הַמָּקוֹם. עַל כֵּן אֲפָרֵשׁ לְךָ אֵיךְ תִּתְנַהֵג בְּמִדַּת
הָעֲנָוָה לָלֶכֶת בָּהּ תָּמִיד: כָּל דְּבָרֶיךָ יִהְיוּ בְּנַחַת,
וְרֹאשְׁךָ כָּפוּף, וְעֵינֶיךָ יַבִּיטוּ לְמַטָּה לָאָרֶץ, וְלִבְּךָ
לְמַעְלָה, וְאַל תַּבִּיט בִּפְנֵי אָדָם בְּדַבֶּרְךָ עִמּוֹ, וְכָל
אָדָם יִהְיֶה גָּדוֹל מִמְּךָ בְּעֵינֶיךָ, וְאִם חָכָם אוֹ עָשִׁיר
הוּא, עָלֶיךָ לְכַבְּדוֹ. וְאִם רָשׁ הוּא, וְאַתָּה עָשִׁיר אוֹ
חָכָם מִמֶּנּוּ, חֲשׁוֹב בְּלִבְּךָ כִּי אַתָּה חַיָּב מִמֶּנּוּ וְהוּא
זַכַּאי מִמְּךָ, שֶׁאִם הוּא חוֹטֵא הוּא שׁוֹגֵג וְאַתָּה מֵזִיד.
בְּכָל דְּבָרֶיךָ וּמַעֲשֶׂיךָ וּמַחְשְׁבוֹתֶיךָ וּבְכָל עֵת, חֲשׁוֹב
בְּלִבְּךָ כְּאִלּוּ אַתָּה עוֹמֵד לִפְנֵי הקב"ה,

---

(1) *Psalms* 93:1. (2) *I Chronicles* 29:12. (3) *Job* 12:20.

that His Presence rests upon you. Indeed, the glory of Hashem fills the universe. — Speak with reverence and awe, like a servant who stands in the presence of his master. Act with restraint in the company of others: If one should call out to you, do not answer with a loud voice, but respond gently — in low tones, as one who stands before his mentor.

Take care to always study Torah diligently so that you will be able to fulfill its commands. When you rise from study, ponder carefully what you have learned; see what there is in it which you can put into practice.

Review your actions every morning and evening, and in this way live all your days in repentance.

Cast external matters from your mind when you stand to pray; carefully prepare your heart in the presence of the Holy One. Purify your thoughts, and ponder your words before you utter them.

Conduct yourself in these ways in all your endeavors for as long as you live. In this way you will surely avoid transgression; your words, actions and thoughts will be flawless. Your prayer will be pure and clear, sincere and pleasing to God, Blessed is He, as it is written: When You prepare their heart [to concentrate], You are attentive [to their prayers.][1]

Read this letter once a week and neglect none of it. Fulfill it, and in so doing, walk with it forever in the ways of Hashem, may He be Blessed, so that you may succeed in your ways and merit the World to Come that lies hidden for the righteous. Every day that you shall read this letter, heaven shall answer your heart's desires . . . Amen, Selah!

---

(1) *Psalms* 10:17.

וּשְׁכִינָתוֹ עָלֶיךָ. כִּי כְבוֹדוֹ מָלֵא הָעוֹלָם, וּדְבָרֶיךָ יִהְיוּ
בְּאֵימָה וּבְיִרְאָה כְּעֶבֶד לִפְנֵי רַבּוֹ, וְתִתְבַּיֵּשׁ מִכָּל
אָדָם, וְאִם יִקְרָאֲךָ אִישׁ אַל תַּעֲנֶנּוּ בְּקוֹל רָם, רַק
בְּנַחַת כְּעוֹמֵד לִפְנֵי רַבּוֹ. וֶהֱוֵי זָהִיר לִקְרוֹת בַּתּוֹרָה
תָּמִיד אֲשֶׁר תּוּכַל לְקַיְּמָהּ, וְכַאֲשֶׁר תָּקוּם מִן הַסֵּפֶר,
תְּחַפֵּשׂ בַּאֲשֶׁר לָמַדְתָּ אִם יֵשׁ בּוֹ דָּבָר אֲשֶׁר תּוּכַל
לְקַיְּמוֹ, וּתְפַשְׁפֵּשׁ בְּמַעֲשֶׂיךָ בַּבֹּקֶר וּבָעֶרֶב, וּבָזֶה יִהְיוּ
כָּל יָמֶיךָ בִּתְשׁוּבָה. וְהָסֵר כָּל דִּבְרֵי הָעוֹלָם מִלְּבָד
בְּעֵת הַתְּפִלָּה, וְהָכֵן לִבְּךָ לִפְנֵי הַמָּקוֹם ב״ה, וְטַהֵר
רַעְיוֹנֶיךָ, וַחֲשׁוֹב הַדִּבּוּר קֹדֶם שֶׁתּוֹצִיאֶנּוּ מִפִּיךָ, וְכֵן
תַּעֲשֶׂה כָּל יְמֵי חַיֵּי הֶבְלֶךָ בְּכָל דָּבָר וְדָבָר וְלֹא
תֶחֱטָא, וּבָזֶה יִהְיוּ דְּבָרֶיךָ וּמַעֲשֶׂיךָ וּמַחְשְׁבוֹתֶיךָ
יְשָׁרִים, וּתְפִלָּתְךָ תִּהְיֶה זַכָּה וּבָרָה וּנְקִיָּה וּמְכֻוֶּנֶת
וּמְקֻבֶּלֶת לִפְנֵי הַמָּקוֹם ב״ה, שֶׁנֶּאֱמַר: תָּכִין לִבָּם
תַּקְשִׁיב אָזְנֶךָ.[1] תִּקְרָא הָאִגֶּרֶת הַזֹּאת פַּעַם אַחַת
בַּשָּׁבוּעַ וְלֹא תִפְחוֹת, לְקַיְּמָהּ וְלָלֶכֶת בָּהּ תָּמִיד אַחַר
הַשֵּׁם יִתְבָּרֵךְ, לְמַעַן תַּצְלִיחַ בְּכָל דְּרָכֶיךָ וְתִזְכֶּה
לְעוֹלָם הַבָּא הַצָּפוּן לַצַּדִּיקִים. וּבְכָל יוֹם שֶׁתִּקְרָאֶנָּה
יַעֲנוּךָ מִן הַשָּׁמַיִם כַּאֲשֶׁר יַעֲלֶה עַל לִבְּךָ לִשְׁאוֹל עַד
עוֹלָם אָמֵן סֶלָה:

The Introductory Verse

שְׁמַע בְּנִי מוּסַר אָבִיךָ, וְאַל תִּטֹּשׁ תּוֹרַת אִמֶּךָ.

Heed, my son, the discipline of your father and do not forsake the guidance of your mother *(Proverbs 1:8).*

✑§ *Parenting: Transmitting the Building Blocks of Character*

This verse emphasizes a parent's responsibility to mold his child's character. Even if one is not capable of teaching his child the actual texts of the Torah — *Chumash*, Mishnah and *Gemara* — he is still obligated to instill within him Torah values and morals.

Parents must be ever cognizant of the fact that *middos* are in a sense hereditary. Just as parents transfer their genes to their offspring and thereby determine their physical characteristics, so they transmit their attitudes, values, and character traits to their children. Indeed, parents who don't control their own anger raise hot-tempered children.

Rabbi Nosson Tzvi Finkel, the "Alter of Slabodka" wrote:

> The son of a good family who stole apples from a cart did not become a thief overnight. The deed has its roots in previous generations. Perhaps his very pious grandfather hid behind the *bimah* of the synagogue in the name of humility, but the act contained a trace of deception (*geneivas daas*) because he was acting more pious than he really was. His scholarly son went a step further and "stole" *chiddushei* Torah from other scholars by reciting them in his own name. The grandson, in turn, became an apple thief.

An entire tractate of the Mishnah is devoted to the study of Jewish ethics. Appropriately, this tractate of moral training is called *'Avos,'* *Fathers.*

Parents should foster in their children a spirit of reverence and awe
for God. The *Ohr HaChaim HaKadosh* (comm. to *Deuteronomy* 31:13)
writes:

> A child must be trained to fear God at the earliest possible
> age. Even if he is too young to begin formal Torah learning, he
> should be trained in the fear of Heaven, because then he will
> remain God fearing for the rest of his life.

Elsewhere, the *Ohr HaChaim* (comm. to *Leviticus* 19:3) writes:

> Holy men have told me that when a person is overwhelmed
> by impure thoughts and his Evil Impulse threatens to entice him
> to sin, there is one powerful preventive device. One should
> project a mental image of one's parents; when one sees them
> before him, the forces of sanctity are reinforced within him and
> he will find within himself the strength to overcome temptation.
> Thus, Potiphar's wife nearly succeeded in seducing Joseph until
> the image of his father Jacob appeared before Joseph, and
> helped him overcome his passion.
>
> This explains the order of the verses of the Torah. First the
> Torah commands: קְדוֹשִׁים תִּהְיוּ, *Be holy!* and immediately
> afterward it commands: *Every man of you shall fear his mother
> and his father*, as if to say, "If you wish to safeguard yourself
> from temptation, fear your parents and picture them standing
> before you."

As mentioned in our introduction, *Ramban* addressed this letter to his
son Nachman. *Ramban* wrote another letter to his son Shlomo, who was
in the service of the Spanish government. Therein, *Ramban* emphasizes
how beneficial it is for a child to always think of his parents' teachings:

> My son, remember me always and let the image of my
> countenance always be before your eyes; let it never depart from
> you. Remove from your heart the desire to do anything that you
> know I despise. Be with me always. Observe the command-
> ments of God and live!

ᵉᔍ *In Reward for Truth*

Shaloh HaKadosh advises parents that if they wish to leave an
indelible imprint on their children, they should place utmost importance

on the quality of honesty. The child who is trained to adopt his parent's code of honor can be trusted to act properly under all circumstances, long after his parents are gone.

Shaloh HaKadosh relates that when he lived in Jerusalem he knew a very pious Sephardic Jew who wouldn't deviate from the truth for anything in this world. This Sephardic *chassid* explained to *Shaloh* that his scrupulous honesty was his father's legacy. When he was a small child his father would shower him with gifts if he would confess his mischievous deeds and admit to the truth. On the other hand his father would punish him severely for telling a lie. The little boy never forgot these lessons.

◄§ True Compassion

It is most appropriate for *Ramban* to begin his letter of moral guidance to his son with the verse, *"Heed, my son, the discipline of your father, and do not forsake the guidance of your mother"* (*Proverbs* 1:8).

Rashi (ibid.) explains that *"the discipline of your father"* refers to the basic texts and rules of God's Torah as recorded in the Oral and Written Law, which were given to Moses at Sinai. *"The guidance of your mother"* refers to the additional fences and safeguards which the Rabbis introduced in every generation, in order to keep the people far from sin.

Harav Mordechai Gifter (the Telshe *Rosh Yeshivah*) makes a fascinating observation: The Sadducees, the Karaites, the reformers, and the secularists who despised the Rabbinic tradition always try to characterize the Sages as heartless, insensitive men who introduced myriads of restrictive laws without any concern for the true needs and feelings of the people. These falsifiers of truth claim that the Torah received by Moses was flexible, and filled with compassion, and that it was the later-day rabbis who transformed Judaism with their "strict, overbearing, inflexible, petrified *halachah.*"

But King Solomon, the wisest of all men, reveals this charge as a vicious libel. He describes the basic text of the Torah as the strict *discipline of your father,* whereas he depicts the safeguards of the Rabbis as the gentle *guidance of your mother.*

Harav Gifter explains this with a parable:

Once there was a boy who had a weakness for good food. Much to his parent's dismay, a non-kosher five-star restaurant opened up right in the middle of their neighborhood. The father knew that his son would be sorely tempted by these culinary delights, so he firmly warned him never to eat in the new restaurant, lest he be severely punished. The mother knew her son better. She realized that if he walked by the display window filled with succulent *treif* delicacies or smelled the odors wafting from the kitchen it would be too much for him to resist, and he would easily succumb to his desires.

So the mother issued a stern warning to her son, which was much harsher than her husband's. "My son, don't you dare go within one block of that *treif* restaurant!! If I catch you anywhere near that place you'll get the whipping of your lifetime!"

Is the mother cruel and heartless? To the contrary. She is more sensitive to her son's weakness and more acutely pained by his potential suffering — it is love and concern that compel her to be stricter.

The same applies to the Torah. The Oral and Written Law given at Sinai are the absolutes, the firm basis of Jewish law forever. They resemble the absolute *"discipline of the father."* However, the Almighty designated the Sages of every generation to act as the "mothers" who guide the Jewish people. It was the Torah that indicated the responsibility of the Sages to establish safeguards to prevent transgression of the commandments (see *Ritva, Rosh Hashanah* 16b; *Chinuch* §36). The compassionate Sages were painfully aware of the shortcomings and weaknesses of their own and future generations. In order to protect their beloved people from sin and its punishment, the Rabbis introduced safeguards which were custom-tailored to the needs of the weaker generations. Thus the strict Rabbinical laws are not at all *heartless*, they are actually *heartwarming* evidence of deep concern and love resembling the love of a mother for her children.

Ramban wrote this personal letter to his son in which he displays sensitivity for the specific spiritual needs of his child. The letter is written with both paternal firmness and maternal feeling. Indeed, this is what the study of *middos* is about, because *middos* literally means *measures*, implying that first we establish absolute rules and principles of conduct, and then we apply them in specific measure to meet the spiritual needs of the individual.

1

תִּתְנַהֵג תָּמִיד לְדַבֵּר כָּל דְּבָרֶיךָ בְּנַחַת
לְכָל אָדָם וּבְכָל עֵת.

Accustom yourself to speak gently
to all people at all times.

&§ *Four Steps to Equanimity*

From these opening remarks of *Ramban's Letter*, the teachers of the
Mussar Movement (*Cheshbono Shel Olam*, p. 20; *Hosair Ka'as
Milibecha*, p. 112) derived important lessons on how to maintain one's
equanimity and peace of mind under all circumstances.

(a) תִּתְנַהֵג תָּמִיד — *Accustom yourself.*

Be prepared. Don't let unnerving situations catch you by surprise.
Before crisis hits, prepare in your mind how you would like to react to
trying situations, and resolve to make every effort not to surrender to
panic or rage. Your resolutions will not come true automatically or
easily, but if you prepare yourself mentally — as a driver thinks about
a possible skid — you will be better able to deal with difficult situations,
as they inevitably arise.

(b) לְדַבֵּר . . . בְּנַחַת — *To speak gently.*

Even in tension-packed situations, even when the atmosphere is
charged with hostility, even when you must confront your enemy, even
when you are obligated to admonish someone for a terrible misdeed
speak gently. Gentle words have more force than crescendos of
indignation.

(c) לְכָל אָדָם — *To all people.*

Treat *all people* with equal respect and sensitivity. React calmly even
to someone who has just insulted you maliciously, and remain calm

even when an irritating nuisance pesters you incessantly. *All people* includes even those whom one usually takes for granted — one's parents, spouse, and children. Be as calm and courteous to your immediate family as you are to your superior or most important client.

(d) בְּכָל עֵת — *At all times.*

Never lose your temper — even when you are exhausted, drained, disappointed, aggravated, shocked, confused, terrified. Even when the whole world seems to be crashing down on your head — keep calm. React slowly and deliberately — and *speak gently.*

◆§ *Protect Your Serenity*

Zealously protect your peace of mind. It is one of your most precious possessions.

> Three people are especially beloved by God: One who does not lose control of his temper, one who does not become drunk, and one who does not demand his full rights (*Pesachim* 113a).
>
> One who carefully guards himself against giving in to anger and avoids any arguments merits that his home is compared to the Holy Temple (*Zohar, Tikkunim* 69:2).

A personal credo from *"Lifelines"* by Rabbi Avi Shulman:

> I am calm, serene, and in total control at all times. I am unaffected by the emotions of others. I will not allow anyone to unnerve me, or project his problems on me. I am clear, assertive, pleasant; I speak in a low voice, never degrading or negative. I do nothing rash, accept no condition unless every financial, organizational, and emotional factor is met, and I can succeed.
>
> I am nice, *but firm;*
> Pleasant, *but resolute;*
> Delightful, *but determined;*
> Cordial, *but tenacious;*
> Respectful, *but unyielding;*
> Gracious, *but immutable;*
>
> I may not be able to control other people or situations, but I can always control my attitude.

◆§ *Peace of Mind — the Key*

Peace of mind is the key to spiritual growth; serenity is the trademark of the person who is truly godly. The person who has trust in the

Almighty is calm and composed, and this is displayed by his soft and gentle manner of speech. The man of faith is soothed by the advice of King David: *Cast upon Hashem your burden and He will sustain you; He will never allow the faltering of the righteous (Psalms 55:23).* The godly person is filled with confidence by the assurance that his Father in Heaven is willing and able to share all of his worries and woes.

On the other hand, one who feels that he alone carries all his burdens on his own shoulders can be overwhelmed by the weight of those responsibilities. Such an attitude leads to strong anxiety and tension.

The anxious person who fails to share his problems with God views his environment as hostile and threatening. He imagines that the entire world demands his attention and reaction — so he shouts back, raising his voice above the roar of the threatening tempest.

Indeed, faith can make a seemingly cruel world less forbidding. In such a world, it is natural for a godly person to speak softly.

◆§ Defusing Crises

King Solomon taught in the Book of *Koheles* (*Ecclesiastes* 9:17), דִּבְרֵי חֲכָמִים בְּנַחַת נִשְׁמָעִים, *The words of the wise, spoken gently, are heard.*

The wise man remains in control under any circumstances. He listens courteously and quietly when others address him [the letters of *listen* can be rearranged to spell *silent*]. He thinks before he speaks, allowing himself a few moments of thought before he offers his calm response. He chooses his words carefully and counts them out sparingly like precious coins.

The wise man relies on the force of his arguments and the merit of his logic. He needs no thunder or drama to intimidate his listeners; strong people do not need strong words.

The *Chazon Ish* once testified that his influence was due to the fact that he was careful with his tone of voice when he advised others.

2

וּבְזֶה תִּנָּצֵל מִן הַכַּעַס.

Gentle speech will protect you
from anger.

◆§ Soothing Anger

מַעֲנֶה רַךְ יָשִׁיב חֵמָה וּדְבַר עֶצֶב יַעֲלֶה אָף, *A soft answer turns away wrath, but a distressing word stirs up anger* (Proverbs 15:1).

Malbim comments that the term חֵמָה, *wrath,* connotes intense inner fury — a deep anger which is concealed from others. אָף, *anger,* however, implies a more superficial rage which is quickly expressed and dissipated. While one provocative remark can kindle anger, even the most intense fury can be soothed by a gentle word.

Even when one cannot help another tangibly, gentle words can still ease pain. The *Chofetz Chaim* advises: If you are approached for a charitable donation or a loan and are unable to help, take care not to show displeasure to the person who has come to you. Rather, by responding to him in a soft and gentle tone, your words may be able to soothe, even if your deeds cannot (*Ahavas Chesed,* Part III, ch. 23).

◆§ The Road to Self-Control

אַל תְּבַהֵל בְּרוּחֲךָ לִכְעוֹס כִּי כַעַס בְּחֵיק כְּסִילִים יָנוּחַ, *Do not be hastily upset, for anger lingers in the bosom of fools* (Ecclesiastes 7:9).

One cannot conquer anger without wisdom.

Wise men throughout the ages have offered practical techniques to maintain self-control. *Reishis Chachmah, Shaar Ha'anavah* (ch. 3) advises:

Set aside a sum of money that you will give away if you allow yourself to be angered. Be sure that the amount you designate is sufficient to force you to think twice before you lose your temper.

If someone has enraged you, try to avoid looking him in the eye while your anger is intense (ibid. ch. 5). In this way, you will more easily control your rage.

שֵׂכֶל אָדָם הֶאֱרִיךְ אַפּוֹ וְתִפְאַרְתּוֹ עֲבֹר עַל פָּשַׁע, *It is a man's good sense to be slow to anger, and his glory to pass over a transgression* (Proverbs 19:11).

Rabbi Menachem Meiri relates the following story:

There was once a righteous king who had but one major fault; he was angered very easily. To overcome this tendency he wrote three lines on a sheet of paper and appointed one of his servants to show it to him whenever he started to grow angry. The first line read: "Always remember that you are merely a creature, and you yourself are not the Creator." The second line read: "Always remember that you are flesh and blood and will eventually perish." The final line read: "Always remember that there will be mercy for you in the future only if you have mercy on others" (*Sefer HaMiddos*, p. 239).

๏ A Lifetime Struggle

Attaining self-control requires great discipline; it would be a mistake to think that a *tzaddik* is of necessity a naturally mild-mannered person. The *Chofetz Chaim*, for example, worked constantly to improve his character. He struggled, prayed and reflected, refining his *middos* until they were sterling. A disciple once hid under a bench in *shul*, hoping to observe the *Chofetz Chaim's* conduct at night. When midnight approached, the elderly *tzaddik* appeared, opened the Holy Ark, and prayed to Hashem to help him overcome feelings of anger.

The world-renowned *Rosh HaYeshivah*, Rav Moshe Feinstein, was known for his pleasant demeanor; even in the most provocative of situations he would avoid an angry response.

When a *yeshivah* student questioned him regarding his serenity however, he made it clear that the quality was not easy to attain, or even natural, to him. "It is years that I have worked on perfecting this trait," he said.

Shortly after World War II, the Shulsinger Bros. Publishing Co. published a fine edition of the Talmud. Rav Moshe was among the first to purchase a set of the expensive volumes.

Once, while using one of the new volumes he momentarily left the room. He had been using a dip pen and a bottle of ink. While he was away, a student unintentionally knocked over the bottle, spilling black ink all over the page.

As the student stood in shame, the *Rosh HaYeshivah* returned to the room. Upon perceiving what had happened, however, Rav Moshe smiled pleasantly. He assured the student that the *Gemara* still looked beautiful and, with a comforting glance, returned to study.

3

שֶׁהִיא מִדָּה רָעָה לְהַחֲטִיא בְּנֵי אָדָם.

Anger is a most serious character flaw which causes one to sin.

◆§ Anger and Idolatry

Anger is not only an individual character trait — it is a barometer of personality as well. A wise man advised: "Before you take someone as your friend, observe him when he is angered. His conduct under pressure will tell you volumes about his true nature" [see *Eruvin* 65b] (*Orchos Tzaddikim* ch. 12).

When a person consistently loses his temper, he loses his rational sense as well. The very basis of his relationship with God can become endangered, for there is nothing to restrain him. Thus, the Talmud (*Shabbos* 105b) states: "The man who loses himself to anger is considered to have worshiped idols."

When a person becomes unrestricted, he approaches idolatry.

Unable to think clearly, the man who is lost in fury loses perspective. The crooked path appears straight; the forbidden seems permissible. Insults, quarreling, and slander are no longer distant from him. Although an otherwise sensitive man, the angered person may in his fury come even to humiliate others publicly. When no longer guided by reason, even the most unspeakable acts can come within reach (*Chofetz Chaim; Chovas Hashmirah*, p. 24).

◆§ Quieted Anger — Its Own Reward

Elijah the prophet said: "If you never come to anger, you will never come to sin" (*Berachos* 29a).

The Talmud (*Pesachim* 66b) stresses the consequences of falling prey to wrath: "Whoever loses his temper — if he is a scholar, he will lose his wisdom; if a prophet, he will lose his holy spirit." Indeed, the Gemara warns that a man's unbridled fury can potentially destroy his life (*Pesachim* 113b).

Sefer Chassidim (655) illustrates how one man who controlled his anger saved himself from destroying his family:

> Once there was a son who was extraordinarily respectful to his father. On his deathbed the father said: "My son, you honored me in my lifetime and now you must honor me after my death. I command you — if you should ever be overcome by anger, hold your anger in *overnight*." After his father's death, the son was forced to embark on a prolonged journey which took him to distant lands for tens of years. Unbeknownst to him, the wife he left behind was expecting his child. After his years of absence, the husband returned home unannounced, hoping to joyously surprise his wife. But as he approached his bed-chamber he saw his wife embracing a handsome young man, a stranger. The husband became fiercely jealous and reached for his dagger — when he suddenly remembered the pledge he made to his father: He must hold in his rage overnight. The next day he was shocked to discover that the young man in his wife's embrace was none other than his own son, the child that his wife had borne during his long absence. The man was thus saved from tragically slaughtering his own family.

◂§ A Weighted Balance

Rambam teaches in *Hilchos De'os* (ch. 2) that a person should balance his personality traits, avoiding the extremes of any one trait. He should endeavor to be strong, yet flexible; compassionate, yet firm. *Rambam* notes however, one exception to his rule: In reference to anger, there is no middle way. A person must strive rather for an opposite extreme, avoiding wrath even in situations where anger is indeed justifiable.

Similarly, *Sefer HaMiddos* (*Shaar Hasinnah*, ch. 5) writes:

> The trait of anger is undeniably evil. It is natural to wild and unclean animals, beasts and birds of prey. The angry man is similar to a viper whose food, the dust of the earth, is available to it wherever the bird travels. So too, the angry man may easily

find cause to become abrasive, regardless of the situation which he finds himself in.

❧ Anger Reaches Outside Itself

Anger does not remain inside itself; it affects those who live around it as well. King Solomon advises: *"Do not associate with a man of temper and do not come near a man of wrath, lest you learn from his ways and endanger your soul"* (*Proverbs* 22:24-25). Anger is indeed contagious. By associating with a short-tempered person one may also come to adopt his nature (*R' S.R. Hirsch, From the Wisdom of Mishlei*, p. 193).

Similarly, it is not only the angry person himself who can be led to transgressions, for one man's anger can bring others to sin also. The Talmud (*Gittin* 6b) warns that a man should be exceedingly careful not to show anger in the presence of his wife, lest she come to desecrate the Sabbath. *Rashi* explains that a wife who lives in fear of her husband's rage may, in order to protect herself, come to light candles or finish cooking after the onset of Shabbos. Indeed, in many ways the repercussions of a man's anger reach far beyond himself.

4

כָּל הַכּוֹעֵס כָּל מִינֵי גֵּיהִנָּם שׁוֹלְטִין בּוֹ.

Whoever flares up in anger is subject to the discipline of Gehinnom.

✑§ Surrender to Rage: Abandoning Restraint

Rabbeinu Nissim (comm. *Nedarim* 22a) interprets this statement as a promise of retribution to the person who surrenders to rage. Anger is dangerous not only in and of itself, but also because of what it can lead to. Loosening the bridle of self-control can often be a first step toward abandoning restraint altogether. As each successive bond is severed, ultimately the bond of belief in God will fall as well. Open and unfettered, the angry man is powerless to avoid sin, and lays himself open to its devastating consequences.

Harav Yerucham Levovitz understands that through anger, the pain of Gehinnom becomes real even in this world. He infers this from King David's words: הֹ' הֶעֱלִיתָ מִן שְׁאוֹל נַפְשִׁי, *HASHEM, You have raised up my soul from the Lower World* (*Psalms* 30:4), which were written while David was yet alive. The burning emotions of anger, depression, and frustration are their own emotional hell (*Daas Chachmah U'Mussar*, vol. III, pp. 20; 252).

Beis Avraham (p. 31) observes that the greatest danger of a hostile disposition is that it prevents others from offering constructive criticism. A person's peers will not point out his faults if they fear a tirade in response. Without criticism to aid him, the easily angered person is more liable to fail in developing other aspects of his character as well.

Sefer Chareidim (*Teshuvah*, ch. 4) writes that the delicate soul, a celestial fragment of the Almighty, cannot tolerate anger. When a man succumbs to uncontrollable rage, his soul in a sense departs, leaving behind a deathly vacuum. One who surrenders to anger thus commits a form of spiritual suicide.

He writes further: If one lost a beautiful flower, it would be madness for him to react by breaking a precious object worth thousands of times more than the small flower. Similarly, the person who loses his temper shatters his peace of mind — a commodity far more precious than the relatively trivial loss which triggered his wrath.

Rav Yisrael Salanter, the founder of the Mussar Movement, was especially aware of anger as a spiritual poison. Once, while he was living in Berlin, a visitor found Rav Yisrael uncharacteristically upset. The visitor inquired as to the source of his troubles. Rav Yisrael answered that two Jews from Kovno had just come to visit, and had reported to him on potentially troublesome changes that were about to be made in the local *Beis Midrash*, where Rav Yisrael used to study.

"Are the changes that bad?" asked the visitor.

"No," answered Rav Yisrael, "but nevertheless, I felt some anger when I was told of them."

"Did you speak to the guests in a way that could have contained an element of insult?"

"God forbid." answered Rav Yisrael. "No one but myself knew of it: certainly you know, however, that when a person gets angry, it is as if he were worshiping idols, and is subject to Divine retribution."

◄§ *Bittersweet Gifts*

A philosopher once commented that: "Most men endure lives of quiet frustration." Unfortunately, many people who display outward composure are consumed by inner turmoil — their hearts overflow with bitter disappointments. With each new experience of life's setbacks, they become more deeply angered.

The Talmud (*Arachin* 16b) suggests an antidote to these feelings. No man is free of sin. Although God has no mercy on those who are thoroughly evil, He acts with compassion towards the bulk of mankind. Instead of overwhelming transgressors with devastating blows, God allows them to experience the consequences of sin gradually and over time. The Talmud cites numerous examples of minor discomforts which may serve as Divine retribution. They include: commissioning a tailor to sew a suit and disliking it, asking for a hot drink and being served a cold one, and reaching into one's pocket to take out three coins but coming up with two. The Talmud concludes:

> If a person goes through forty days without experiencing any pain or slight discomfort he should be concerned, lest he receive all of his reward and pleasure in This World and suffering awaits him in the future. Even these apparently trivial discomforts are meaningful. They are indeed God's bittersweet gifts.

The Midrash (*Bamidbar Rabbah* 9:2) suggests that one develop a positive attitude towards the losses which occur in the course of normal life.

> Always be willing to forgive the mishaps which occur in your home. When someone breaks a bottle of expensive wine, if you react with compassion — God Himself will repay your loss.

5

וְכַאֲשֶׁר תִּנָּצֵל מִן הַכַּעַס
תַּעֲלֶה עַל לִבְּךָ מִדַּת הָעֲנָוָה.

Once you have distanced yourself from anger, the quality of humility will enter your heart.

◆§ Humility — a Key to Inner Strength

The masters of Mussar teach that the angry person suffers from a sense of inferiority. Rav Shlomo Wolbe makes the following observation (*Alei Shur*, Volume I p. 42):

> One who craves attention from others has not yet found himself; he is unaware of his true worth. Lacking self-esteem, he depends on the opinion of others. He hungers for their praise, for without their appreciation he feels worthless. When people fail to applaud him he becomes helpless, and therefore, hostile and angry.

Thus, the angry man cannot be a humble man. His anger demonstrates his resentment that the events of life have failed to conform with his expectations. His pride is wounded, and he seeks to compensate his esteem by putting his personal wants and opinions before others. His anger thus leads him to an ultimate display of arrogance.

In distancing himself from this anger and resentment, the serene man subdues arrogance, and in time, is led towards true humility. In this he seeks to strive for perfect הִשְׁתַּוּוּת, *equilibrium:* Ultimately it makes no difference to the humble man whether he is praised or insulted byothers.

others. His self-esteem comes solely from within himself (*Chovos HaLevavos* 5:5).

◦§ The Unattainable Goal

R' Chaim Shmulevitz, observed a curious phenomenon in relation to the pursuit of glory: When a pompous person fails to earn the approval of even an insignificant person, he is so sorely vexed that all the honor he has so far attained seems worthless in his eyes. Even at the height of his glory the honor-seeker is troubled if even one person fails to show the respect which he demands. Although physical desires have saturation points, the desire for recognition has no real limits — it can never be fully fulfilled. Indeed since the thirst for honor is based on an internal lack of self-worth, no amount of outside praise can truly quench it. Thus, while the humble person finds serenity, one who seeks honor and recognition cultivates a life of inevitable frustration (*Sichos Mussar*; Rav Chaim Shmulevitz, 5733; essay #17).

◦§ Abandon Yourself

In analyzing the word *simchah* — joy — one finds at its root, *machah* — to erase (מחה – שמחה). If one truly wishes to rejoice, he must first abandon the conscious desire to place his own needs first. In a sense, he must forget about himself.

> A pious man was asked, "What was the happiest moment in your entire life?" He replied, "I was once traveling on a ship. Because of my poverty, I was assigned the worst quarters imaginable — in the lowest hold, together with the cargo. A group of rich merchants was also on board. Once, as I lay in my berth, one of the merchants who had come down to the hold dumped his waste on me. Apparently, I seemed so despicable in his eyes that he simply pretended that I wasn't there. I was shocked by the man's audacity; nevertheless, I was pleased to find that I felt no anger at being offended. When I realized how indifferent I was to my own prestige, I was truly overcome with joy. I recognized I had achieved a level of genuine humility" (*Rambam* comm. to *Mishnah Avos* 4:4).

6

שֶׁהִיא מִדָּה טוֹבָה מִכָּל הַמִּדּוֹת טוֹבוֹת.
Humility — This sterling quality is the finest of all admirable traits.

This statement parallels a similar clause in *Rambam's* (Maimonides) ethical will: "Humility is the ladder which leads to sublime heights. Remember: There is no ornament as attractive as humility."

◆§ *The Receptive Crystal*

Tomer Devorah (ch. II) sees humility as the key to attaining the gamut of excellent character traits. In a sense, humility can be seen as a sort of spiritual "superconductor." Electricity does not flow smoothly through all metal. Impurities in some offer resistance to electric flow, and cause energy to be lost. Other pure metals, however, can act as "superconductors" — allowing currents to pass through them smoothly, with no energy loss. Thus, just as certain pure metals conduct electricity without offering resistance, so too man may refine himself into a pure vessel through which Divine energy flows freely. By internalizing a humble nature, man filters the clouding element of self-absorption, and becomes crystalline; attuned and receptive to the desires of his Maker.

◆§ *Humility's Hallmarks*

Shevet Mussar (ch. 17) outlines several behavior patterns which identify genuine humility:

□ **Speaking Gently** — The humble man speaks gently even to those who are dependent upon him — family, employees, and the poor of his town. He treats all men and women with equal respect and honesty.

□ **Accepting Praise** — If others heap undeserved praise upon him, he will not hesitate to deflect it. However, even when he is rightly honored, the humble man is genuinely abashed. Although justifiably pleased with his accomplishments, he is aware that they represent a fraction of his potential; he has still left much undone.

□ **Response to Success** — Genuine humility increases in proportion to the humble person's success. Even as God bestows great fortune upon him, the humble man does not grow proud. He responds to success by increasing his devotion to God and his dedication to the needs of others.

□ **Making Amends** — If he has an argument with another, the humble person does everything in his power to swiftly make amends. He begs forgiveness of his antagonist.

□ **Avoiding Revenge** — The humble person never takes revenge. Even when viciously attacked, he is able to forgive his assailant, and in time is able to erase the incident from his mind.

□ **Acceptance** — The humble person can accept suffering without breaking; his intense love for his Creator helps him absorb the harshest of life's blows.

The humble man merits Divine assistance, as King David says: יַדְרֵךְ עֲנָוִים בַּמִּשְׁפָּט וִילַמֵּד עֲנָוִים דַּרְכּוֹ, *He leads the humble with justice and will teach the humble His way* (Psalms 25:9). God assists the humble in achieving spiritual perfection.

⊸§ *The Empty Coach*

Extraordinary humility has been a hallmark of Torah leaders since the beginning of our history. Moshe Rabbeinu, one of the most accomplished men who ever lived, is described by the Torah as, . . . *very humble, more so than all the men on the face of the earth* (Numbers 12:3). His example has served as a model for others throughout history:

> All of the Jews of Warsaw came to greet the two greatest scholars of their generation. Tens of thousands of men, women, and children lined the streets to pay honor to Rabbi Akiva Eiger of Posen and Rabbi Yaakov Lorberbaum of Lisa, who had come to visit. As the crowd surged forward, the men of the city unhitched the horses. In a profound show of respect to the Torah scholars, they themselves grabbed hold of the wooden shafts and began pulling the coach forward.

Inside the coach, the two giants of Israel sat in opposite corners, each engrossed in their thoughts. Rabbi Eiger pondered: Wasn't the great Rav Yaakov of Lisa in the coach? Surely this magnificent welcome must be for him! Rabbi Eiger yearned to take part in this *mitzvah* of honoring the Torah. He slipped quietly out of the door on his side of the wagon and joined those pulling the vehicle.

In the other corner, Rav Yaakov was lost in similar thoughts. It was clear to him that all this honor was intended for Rabbi Akiva Eiger. He too wished to join in this demonstration of respect. Rav Yaakov slipped out of his door and also joined the throngs drawing the coach.

And so the multitudes continued their tumultuous reception for the rabbis, unaware that they were pulling a coach empty of its passengers, but filled to the brim with humility.

Sefer HaMiddos predicts: When the world witnesses a renaissance of the quality of humility, mankind can begin to expect the arrival of the Messiah (see *Sanhedrin* 98a). *Menoras HaMeor* adds that at that time, the humble folk will be hailed as true heroes of humanity, as it is written: כִּי רוֹצֶה ה׳ בְּעַמּוֹ יְפָאֵר עֲנָוִים בִּישׁוּעָה, *When HASHEM shows favor to His nation, He will glorify the humble at the time of salvation* (*Psalms* 149:4).

7

עֵקֶב עֲנָוָה יִרְאַת ה'.
וּבַעֲבוּר הָעֲנָוָה תַּעֲלֶה עַל לִבְּךָ מִדַּת הַיִּרְאָה.

On the heels of humility comes the fear of God *(Proverbs 22:4).* Through humility, the fear of God will intensify in your heart.

৵§ Humility and Fear of God

Genuine humility is synonymous with fear of God — such fear is essentially nothing other than a sense of surrender to the Almighty. The arrogant man harbors illusions of self-sufficiency and independent power. The truly humble person, however, recognizes that God is his only real source of strength. He surrenders his independent self to God, and seeks to merge his will with that of his Creator's.

Chovos Halevavos (Shaar Ahavas Hashem 2, chapter 6) relates that a pious man was once found sleeping in the wilderness. He was asked: "What caused you to remain calm, and to endure the dread of lions and other wild beasts?" The pious man replied: "I stand wholly before the Almighty God, in whose presence I am fearful to fear anything other than He Himself."

The *Jerusalem Talmud (Shabbos* 1:3) demonstrates the interrelationship between humility and fear of God.

Rav Yitzchak bar Elazar taught:

> The quality which wisdom considers to be its crowning glory [i.e., its most significant achievement], humility considers to be no more than the heel of its shoe [i.e., an incidental accomplish-

ment]. Of wisdom it says: רֵאשִׁית חָכְמָה יִרְאַת ה', *The beginning of wisdom is the fear of HASHEM* (*Psalms* 111:10), [i.e., one cannot begin to comprehend Divine wisdom without actively striving for fear of heaven]. But in reference to humility it says: עֵקֶב עֲנָוָה יִרְאַת ה', *On the heels of humility comes the fear of God* (*Proverbs* 22:4) [i.e., through humility, one is naturally filled with reverence and awe for the Almighty].

In light of this, *Cheshbono Shel Olam* (p. 22) observes that the scholar who amasses knowledge but has no fear of his Creator is similar to an emperor who struts about with a magnificent crown on his head while he yet remains barefoot.

◦§ A Concentrated Awareness

Rambam (*Hilchos Yesodei HaTorah* 2:2) shows how a heightened awareness of God's presence fills one with a feeling of humility.

How does a person acquire love and fear of God? When he contemplates God's handiwork, and analyzes His amazing and wondrous creations, he witnesses God's wisdom which has no measure or limit. Immediately he is filled with love and praise for God and yearns to know Him. Such thoughts fill the person with a profound sense of awe; he recoils in the realization that he is nothing more than a frail creature standing in the presence of the Almighty, the source of perfect wisdom. This is as King David said: *When I behold the heavens, the work of Your fingers, the moon and the stars which You have set in place . . . what is the frail human that You should remember him? And what is the son of mortal man that You should be mindful of him?* (*Psalms* 8:4,5).

Ultimately, it is the acute awareness of God's presence that brings one to true humility.

◦§ Humility Draws on Strength

Rav Yechezkel Levenstein (*Koveitz Sichos* pp. 48-51) warns that humility should never be confused with timidity. The timid person, who indiscriminately seeks to please, acts from weakness rather than from strength. Like the angry man, one who is servile is more than likely insecure: his actions stem less from an awareness of God than from a deep mistrust of himself.

The genuinely humble spirit, however, is an exalted one. His security with himself allows him to understand that alone and without God, his existence is insignificant. As he draws close to his Creator, his heart overflows with quiet bliss.

⋄§ An Ultimate Yardstick

וְהָאִישׁ מֹשֶׁה עָנָו מְאֹד מִכֹּל הָאָדָם אֲשֶׁר עַל פְּנֵי הָאֲדָמָה, *And the man Moses was exceedingly humble, more than any man on the face of the earth* (*Numbers* 12:3). It is inconceivable that Moses, the leader and redeemer of millions of Jews, could feel insignificant. He performed the awesome miracles which humbled Egypt's empire, and stood upon Mt. Sinai as the very heavens opened and the Master of the universe revealed Himself. Clearly, Moses was aware of his greatness.

The *Telshe Rav, Rav Yosef Leib Bloch*, explained that one can soar to the pinnacles of success and still remain humble: Humility depends, more than anything else, upon the personal yardstick one chooses. If a six-foot man measures himself against one who stands at five feet, he can boast of his height. However, if he measures himself against the height of the sun, ninety-three-million miles above him, his height seems negligible.

Similarly, men wax proud only when they measure themselves against smaller men. When one measures himself against the infinite and eternal Creator, he understands his own relative insignificance. Thus, precisely because Moses achieved such a tangible closeness to God, was he humbled more than any man to have walked the earth. One's greatness as a person depends perhaps, on the degree to which he can truly perceive his Creator's presence, and make such an ultimate yardstick a reality for himself.

8

כִּי תִתֵּן אֶל לִבְּךָ תָּמִיד,
מֵאַיִן בָּאתָ, וּלְאָן אַתָּה הוֹלֵךְ,
וְשָׁאַתָּה רִמָּה וְתוֹלֵעָה בְּחַיֶּיךָ, וְאַף כִּי בְמוֹתָךְ.

The fear of God will intensify in your heart, for you will always be aware from where you have come and to where you are destined to go. You will realize that in life you are as frail as the maggot or the worm — all the more so in death.

This statement is based on the Mishnah in *Avos* (3:1) which offers three deterrents to sin.

> Akavya ben Mehalalel said: "Consider three things and you will not fall into the grip of sin. Know from where you come, to where you are going, and before Whom you are destined to be judged and called to account."

Mesilas Yesharim (ch. 23) explains:

> All of the above thoughts counteract pride and promote humility. When a man ponders his earthly nature and lowly beginnings, he sees little reason to feel proud ... Man's position is similar to that of a swineherd who has attained lordship: only as long as he remembers his early days will it be impossible for him to become arrogant.

The source of humility is alluded to once again in *Avos* 4:4: Rabbi Levitas of Yavneh said: "Be exceedingly humble in spirit, for the anticipated end of mortal man is the worm."

It is difficult for man to cast off the illusion that he will live forever. Yet to the extent that he succeeds, he will attain humility:

Some of the members of the fabulously wealthy Rothschild family were known for their piety. One of the Rothschilds would disappear from his bank office every day at noon and return after an hour's absence. For years, no one knew where he went, until finally a curious clerk followed Rothschild's carriage on its daily drive outside the city limits. When the carriage reached the Jewish cemetery, Rothschild emerged. To the astonishment of the clerk, the wealthy man had discarded his customary frock coat and silk top hat, and instead was wearing *tachrichim*, the white shrouds of the dead. Rothschild stepped down into an opened grave and laid down flat and motionless for a long period, repeating over and over again the words of Rabbi Levitas: "Be exceedingly humble in spirit, for the anticipated end of mortal man is the worm."

Once I accompanied my father-in-law, the Telshe *Rosh HaYeshivah*, HaRav Mordecai Gifter. After he visited the gravesites on *Har Hazeisim*, he told me of mystical texts which write that preparing one's burial place in one's lifetime is considered meritorious, and helps one secure a longer life in the heavenly accounting. Indeed, when death starts to become a tangible reality, one is more likely to improve the spiritual quality of his days, and thus merit long life.

ৎ§ A Night in the Graveyard

The Talmud (*Berachos* 5a) teaches:

A person should seize every opportunity to do battle with his Evil Inclination. If he triumphs, all is well; yet if he at first fails, he should engage in vigorous Torah study. If this subdues his desire for evil, all is well; yet if it does not, let him then recite the Shema — the credo of the Jewish faith. If he then succeeds, all is well, but if he does not, as a last resort, let him picture the day of death. This vision will undoubtedly destroy evil's allure.

The Talmud (*Berachos* 18a) tells of a certain *chassid* who, on Rosh Hashanah's eve, gave a precious coin to a beggar. The year before had been one of severe famine and poverty, and the *chassid's* wife felt her husband should have kept the coin for his own needs. They quarreled over the incident, and the *chassid* became angry. That night, he inexplicably left his home to spend the night of Rosh Hashanah sleeping in the local graveyard.

Rabbi Yisrael Salanter (*Ohr Yisrael*, ch. 26) explains that the *chassid* recognized that his anger represented a shortcoming in his character: the genuinely humble person accepts life's unpleasantries with serenity. Thus, the *chassid* felt unprepared to be examined by the Almighty on the morrow, the Day of Judgment, while still harboring such a serious flaw in his nature — hence, he slept in the cemetery to overwhelm his pride quickly. Nothing so wholly convinces a man of his own frailty as contemplating his inevitable mortality.

9

וְלִפְנֵי מִי אַתָּה עָתִיד לִתֵּן דִּין וְחֶשְׁבּוֹן,
לִפְנֵי מֶלֶךְ הַכָּבוֹד.

It is this sense of humility which reminds you of the One before Whom you will be called for judgment — the King of Glory.

◄§ Channeling Energy

This statement is also based on the words of Akavya ben Mehalalel cited above (*Mishnah Avos* 3:1), who concludes his lists of deterrents to sin with this advice:

> Remember before Whom you are destined to be summoned for judgment and accounting — before the King of kings, the Holy One, Blessed is He!

The *Vilna Gaon* questions why the *tanna* repeats himself by using *two* terms to describe the final reckoning: דִּין, *judgment*, and חֶשְׁבּוֹן, *accounting*.

He explains that *judgment* is rendered for a sinful act which was actually committed, while *accounting* is an additional reckoning that will be made of the positive deeds which could have been accomplished with the energy used to sin. One will be called to task not only for sin itself, but for the tragic misuse of his precious time and energy.

In this way, Rabbi Yisrael Salanter once chastised a man who physically attacked his neighbor. The rabbi informed the ruffian that he had committed two serious sins: "First, you struck and harmed a fellow human being. Second, the energy you spent to accomplish this crime could have been used constructively. This waste is a grave offense as well."

⋙ Laundering the Royal Robes

Rabbi Chaim of Volozhin (*Ruach Chaim*, *Avos* 3:1) cites *Shabbos* 125b which presents a parable of a king who lent his garb to two groups of men. One group carelessly returned the clothes to the king soiled, battered and tarnished. The wise men, however, gave everything back in better condition than they received it. The royal robes were laundered and sparkling white and the regalia polished to a dazzling shine. The Talmud concludes that God, too, lends every human being a fragment of His glory, a celestial soul. Fools sully their souls with the blemishes of transgression, while the wise polish them with *mitzvos*. On the Day of Reckoning transgressors will be summoned to *judgment* for tarnishing their Divine soul and will be subjected to an *accounting* for failing to enhance them.

⋙ The Two-Fold Effect

Beis HaLevi (*Parashas Noach*) observes a two-fold effect in every sin. Wrongdoing both defiles a man, and exerts an influence on others who are led to follow the example of the transgressor. This is especially true of one who enjoys a position of prestige. If he acts scrupulously, his example is a shining one, yet if he corrupts his position, who can tell how many multitudes are led astray by his influence?

Indeed, the effect of one man's wrongdoings is not limited to the present — it continues in the future, as well: His children and grandchildren learn from him also. It is this indirect, yet wide-ranging influence of sin which is also brought to judgment in the day of final *accounting*. [See *Chiddushei HaGriz Al HaTorah* (stencil), number 151, and *Meshech Chachmah*, *Parashas Vayeira* 18:28 and end of *Parashas Nitzavim*.]

⋙ Picturing the Day of Judgment

Mesillas Yesharim (ch. 23) vividly illustrates the advice of Akavya ben Mehalalel to remember the Day of Judgment:

> One should paint a sharp mental picture of what he will experience [after death] when he is presented to the Heavenly Court [for judgment] in view of the Celestial Legions. The

defendant will stand in front of the King of Kings, the ultimate source of sanctity and purity. The Almighty is surrounded by ministering angels, who carry out His wishes with absolute perfection. He, the defendant, will stand exposed to their intense scrutiny ... painfully aware of the worst of his actions. Overwhelmed, will the defendant be able to raise his head? Will he dare open his mouth? If the court shall ask: "Have you lost your tongue? Where is the honor and glory that you have prided yourself in your lifetime?" What shall he answer? How can anyone respond to this rebuke?

If one would for even a moment form a true, forceful impression of this idea, his pride would take flight from him, never to return.

ᐁᔥ Silent Witnesses

The Talmud (*Taanis* 11a) describes how evidence will be presented to the Heavenly Tribunal for the final judgment:

One who thinks, "I can sin in the privacy of my home, who will testify against me?" is mistaken. The very stone walls and wooden beams, which now conceal, will cry out later and condemn his hidden sins ... Indeed, a person's own soul which resides within him will bear witness of his wrongdoings. As one passes on to eternal rest, the deeds he performed throughout his lifetime will precede him on his last journey. When the court issues its verdict the one who is overwhelmed with sin has no choice but to attach his signature to a written confession and humbly accept the sentence, saying, "This verdict is indeed true and just."

10

וְכַאֲשֶׁר תַּחְשׁוֹב אֶת כָּל אֵלֶּה,
תִּירָא מִבּוֹרְאֶךָ וְתִשְׁמוֹר מִן הַחֵטְא.

**After you give serious thought to these
ideas you will stand in awe of your Creator
and will be guarded against sin.**

◆§ A Perpetual Need

The Torah commands: אֶת ה׳ אֱלֹהֶיךָ תִּירָא, *You shall fear HASHEM your
God* (*Deuteronomy* 10:20). To live in awe of God is a positive
commandment, one of the six hundred and thirteen *mitzvos*. The
mitzvah is constant: It applies in all places at all times; every moment of
the day and night. The obligation devolves upon every member of the
human race, Jew and gentile alike.

Although the *mitzvah* applies at all times, it is especially important to
feel the awe of God in situations that try one's moral stamina. It is easier
to overcome temptation when one realizes that God watches human
actions, and mournfully records every transgression (*Sefer HaChinuch;
Mitzvah* 432).

◆§ The Buried Treasure

*And now, Israel, what does HASHEM your God ask of you — only that
you fear HASHEM your God* . . . (*Deuteronomy* 10:12).

Mesillas Yesharim cites numerous sources which demand that one
exert effort to learn how to serve God with pure intent. The most
essential ingredient, he writes, is striving to sense a genuine fear of
heaven:

King Solomon stated: *If you seek it out as you seek silver and search for it as you search for buried treasures — then will you comprehend the fear of HASHEM* (Proverbs 2:4,5). He does not say: "Then you will comprehend philosophy; then you will master astronomy; then you will understand medicine; then you will grasp the meaning of the fine points of law." These pursuits, while commendable, are not the ultimate purposes of life. It is only comprehension of fear of God which truly warrants incessant study and research.

Mesillas Yesharim suggests that one set aside a specific period of time in his daily schedule to contemplate a personal approach to the fear of God. He also describes a process of acquiring fear of transgression (ch. 25):

> One should constantly make himself aware that the Divine Presence is found everywhere, and the Holy One, Blessed is He, carefully watches everyone and everything, great and small. Nothing is hidden from His eyes ... When one truly lives with this awareness, he is filled with awe. He genuinely fears acting in a manner which is not in accordance with the wishes of the Almighty.

◄§ Reverence and Awe: An Active Pursuit

Rav Yitzchak Blazer, fondly known as Rav Itzele Peterberger, observes in his masterpiece *Ohr Yisrael* (*Shaarei Ohr*, ch. 2) that, by nature, men are easily frightened. Wherever man turns, he finds himself surrounded by either real or imaginary danger. He is afraid of crime and of competition; afraid of the future and the unknown. He fears failure, sickness, and poverty; pain and death. Indeed, the list has almost no end.

Thus it is curious: If man is a being prone to fear, why does he not also live in awe and trepidation of the most powerful force in the world — the Omnipotent God, Master of the Universe? But lo, in his daily life man seems not to take notice of his Creator at all! Even those who scrupulously follow the dictates of Torah and *mitzvos*, as a whole, seem not overly concerned about sins they commit time and time again.

Rav Yitzchak Blazer explains that man's lack of natural fear of God is indeed unfathomable; yet this strange phenomenon is nonetheless the result of God's perfect design. The Creator Himself purposely plucked fear of God from man's heart so that humanity could enjoy its most precious privilege — the gift of בְּחִירָה חָפְשִׁית, free will. If man was overwhelmed by a natural and instinctive dread of the Almighty, he would unthinkably choose good. Evil would not be an option at all.

Thus, by Divine decree, man does *not* fear God instinctively. Yet, man *can* acquire fear of God intellectually. By actively seeking to recognize God's dominance over every phase of life, man slowly fills his heart with reverence and awe. It is only by this active and forceful pursuit that he becomes imbued with fear of God — there is no other way. Indeed, *if you seek it out as you seek silver and search for it as you search for buried treasures — then will you comprehend the fear of* HASHEM (*Proverbs* 2:4,5).

11

וּבְמִדּוֹת הָאֵלֶּה תִּהְיֶה שָׂמֵחַ בְּחֶלְקֶךְ.

Once you have acquired
these fine qualities
you will indeed be happy with your lot.

⊷§ Finding Contentment: The Process

The Mishnah (*Avos* 4:1) teaches that a truly rich person is "one who is satisfied with his portion." The *Tanna*, however, stops short of offering guidance on how to acquire such satisfaction. Here, in his ethical work, *Ramban* systematically outlines the process of achieving contentment. First, he writes, one must remove anger from his heart. Serenity is impossible if one is easily agitated. Yet, even after conquering anger, if one remains proud — continually seeking new glory — he similarly can never be satisfied. Thus, humility becomes a vital component in the quest for peace of mind as well.

The humble person also achieves contentment through his belief that God controls all of life's events. One who believes that his affairs are controlled by chance feels cheated; despair follows quickly. If he understands that God is close to his daily life, however, he trusts in his Creator's fairness, even when events seem beyond his mortal comprehension. He is content in the knowledge that God will deal with him justly.

⊷§ Serenity Despite Travail

Chofetz Chaim (*Al HaTorah Parshas Vaeschanan* 6:3) asks how a poor and sick person can be expected to be satisfied with his lot. He provides the following illustration: A diamond cutter requires a delicate and expensive saw to cut his gems. The lumberjack, too, needs a saw to cut his logs — but his instrument is large and rough. Although the diamond saw is more expensive, if the lumberjack were to envy the beautiful tool and yearn to use it for his craft, he would be a fool: The saw, albeit valuable, is entirely unsuited for his needs.

Similarly, the Almighty created every human being with a different mission in life, and invested each person with unique physical and emotional tools to carry out his mission. The rich man is supplied with wealth with which to serve God through philanthropy. On the other hand, God provides each afflicted person with the strength to withstand suffering: The sick man serves God by struggling with his illness, yet accepting his pain with serene faith. Thus, poverty can be the bittersweet tool of a man's life mission. Although the poor man may wish for wealth, it is his ability to deal valiantly with his lot that is his key to spiritual perfection. Hence, the person who comes to recognize his true mission in God's world can become genuinely satisfied with the "tools" that are *his* portion and no one else's.

◆§ A City of Happiness — A State of Mind

Rabbeinu Asher in his *Orchos Chaim* (#66) makes this recommendation for developing a contented frame of mind:

> Desire that which your Maker desires for you, and rejoice in the portion He has chosen for you. When you pray, ask for only one thing — that God inspire you to follow His teachings. As for everything else, *Cast upon HASHEM your burden and He will sustain you (Psalms 55:23).*

Rav Avraham Pam, *Rosh HaYeshivah* of Mesivta Torah Vodaath, often quotes an old saying: "People search desperately all over the word to find a 'city of happiness' — not realizing that it can only be found in a 'state of mind.'"

◆§ In the Embrace of the Creator

In his *Psalms*, King David shares with us his secret of serenity: *HASHEM is my allotted portion and my share, You guide my destiny. Portions have fallen to me in pleasant places, indeed, my estate was lovely to me. I will bless HASHEM who has advised me ... (Psalms 16:5-7).*

David was one of the most colorful personalities in Jewish history. He was a powerful king, a victorious warrior, an inspired composer and a sagacious lawgiver. Yet, David avowed that all his achievements were dwarfed by his progress towards his ultimate goal, establishing an intimate relationship with God. Ecstatically, David sings a song of gratitude. Indeed, a mortal can experience no greater delight than to sense the embrace of the Immortal Creator.

12

וְכַאֲשֶׁר תִּתְנַהֵג בְּמִדַּת הָעֲנָוָה לְהִתְבּוֹשֵׁשׁ מִכָּל אָדָם וּלְהִתְפַּחֵד מִמֶּנּוּ.

When your actions display genuine humility — when you stand meekly before man, and fearfully before God.

✑ Honoring God — Honoring Others

Rav Nosson Tzvi Finkel, known as "the Alter of Slabodka" (1849-1928), constantly emphasized that all men are precious, for they are made in the image of God. When one showers others with kindness and respect, he thus also honors God Himself. The first resolution recorded in "the Alter's" spiritual diary was "to try to be extremely careful of my fellow man's honor; with patience, with a soft answer, never once to get excited ... to find ways daily — at the very least weekly — of benefiting my friends."

✑ An Everyday Striving

Mesillas Yesharim (ch. 22) writes that although God has endowed every individual with unique abilities, one should not become unduly proud on their account. Each advantage was meant to be shared:

> One who is wealthy may rejoice in his lot, but at the same time he must help those in need: If one is strong, he must assist the weak. The situation of the world is similar to a large household where there are many different servants assigned to different tasks. Each servant must fulfill his own appointed chore if the affairs and needs of the household are to be managed properly. There is really no room for pride here.

Further on, the *Mesillas Yesharim* develops an axiom to monitor one's response to fortune:

> As one's wealth increases, his pride should wane.
>
> His situation is similar to that of the beggar who accepts gifts of kindness, yet is also humbled because of them. The more he receives, the greater his feeling of indebtedness. Thus, King David reacts to God's kindness by saying: *How can I repay HASHEM for all His kindness to me? (Psalms* 116:12).

In addition to being a giant in Torah knowledge, Rav Moshe Feinstein was also a paragon of piety and wonderful *middos*. Indeed, someone once asked Rav Moshe in what merit he had become so revered by all Jews. He replied, "I have never knowingly caused any hurt to another human being."

His respect for others manifested itself on a daily level. One man recalled how Rav Moshe had once failed to notice him as he walked by. Ten steps later, Rav Moshe turned around and came back, greeted the man, and then — to make up for the oversight — spent some time conversing with him.

One day, as Rav Moshe walked through the lobby of his apartment building, a woman held the front door open for him. The next day, Rav Moshe was in the lobby and noticed the woman approaching the door. This time he rushed over to hold the door for her. "No, no!" she protested, but to no avail.

◆§ Erasing the Traces of Arrogance

After concluding an address to a gathering on the East Side, Rav Moshe quickly made his way toward the exit. As he neared the door, the chairman of the gathering introduced the next speaker — a respected rav of an East Side congregation. Rav Moshe stopped at the door, turned back, and retook his seat for the duration of the rav's address. He feared that some might misinterpret his exit as a lack of regard for the rav, certainly not his intention.

Someone who assisted Rav Moshe for a number of years once asked him, "Why does the *Rosh Yeshivah* permit phone calls to disturb his learning during the day — would it not be more practical to accept calls at specific hours only?"

Rav Moshe replied, "There is a trace of arrogance in telling someone that I cannot be disturbed and he must call me back at my convenience. That is not for me."

After concluding a meeting, Rav Moshe and Rav Yaakov Kamenetzky stood in discussion with one another for a moment before entering a waiting car. As they took their seats, R' Yaakov chose to sit next to the driver while R' Moshe seated himself in the back. After Reb Moshe alighted from the car, Rav Yaakov explained to the driver the reason for the delay: "We were discussing who would be getting off first. That person, we decided, should sit in the back. Were he to sit in the front, you would be left alone there when he left the car, with your remaining passenger in the back. It would have looked as if you were nothing more than a chauffeur."

13

אָז תִּשְׁרֶה עָלֶיךָ רוּחַ הַשְּׁכִינָה, וְזִיו כְּבוֹדָהּ,
וְחַיֵּי עוֹלָם הַבָּא.

Then the spirit of God's Presence
will rest upon you, as will the splendor
of His glory; you will live the life
of the World to Come.

◆§ The World to Come in This World

This is perhaps the most intriguing statement in *Ramban's* letter. Here, the author holds a glimpse of an entirely new level of life — an other-worldly existence which one actually experiences here on earth: it Yiddish it is known as *Olam Haba oif die velt,* "The World to Come in this world."

In *Psalms* 27:4 King David writes: *One thing I asked of* HASHEM, *that I shall seek: that I dwell in the House of* HASHEM *all the days of my life.* According to *Rambam* (*Hilchos Teshuvah* 8:4), the *House of Hashem* does not refer to a place in this world, but rather to the bliss of the World to Come. *HaRav Mordecai Gifter* שליט״א asks: If this phrase refers to the Hereafter, how can David ask to dwell in the House of Hashem *"all the days of my life"* — during his mortal existence? Rav Gifter thus cites this as proof to the words of the *Ramban's* letter that one who perfects his personality can experience the delight of the World to Come during his lifetime as well.

◆§ Transcending the Trivial

How does one get there? *Ramban* maps the route earlier in his letter. The key is self-discipline and refinement of character. One who trains himself to be gentle, humble and at peace with the world rises above the trivial pursuits which bind the common man. Inspired by fear of God, this person lives a life of unparalleled quality: Although his feet are planted on the ground, his heart and mind soar to effortless heights.

Ramban alludes to this goal elsewhere in his writings. In his commentary on the verse: *Love HASHEM your God, walk in His ways and cling tightly to Him (Deuteronomy* 11:22), *Ramban* explains that when a person is filled with love of God, he thinks about Him always. Even when seemingly involved in the mundane pursuits of life, he who loves God will not allow himself to be distracted: He speaks business with his tongue and lips, while his heart remains concentrated elsewhere, upon his beloved Creator. People of this stature bind their souls, even while they walk on earth, to the bond of eternal life; their bodies become a palace for the Divine Presence.

◆§ Glimpsing the Divine

Rabbi Avrohom Yeshaya Karelitz, the *Chazon Ish*, paints a poetic portrait of the spiritual heights one can reach when he succeeds in transcending the mundane. In his treatise on *Emunah U'Bitachon* (ch. I section 9), he writes:

> When a person elevates himself to the point that he is able to truly sense the presence of the Almighty God, he is filled with an ecstasy which has no bounds. His soul basks in delight, as earthly desires simply become unimportant. His delicate soul is wrapped in a sacred embrace.
>
> When a mortal enters this realm of sanctity, a new world opens before his eyes. One can live in this world and yet actually, for a brief period, experience angelic ecstasy: All mundane pleasures melt into nothingness in the face of his celestial bliss. There is no greater testimony to the Divine origins of man than this unique encounter of the soul with its spiritual source.

Elsewhere, the *Chazon Ish* repeats this idea in a letter:

> When one is privileged to know the Torah, his intellect, like a seed in the furrow of a field, unites with his knowledge and they become a single entity. He walks among people and seems to the superficial observer to be an ordinary person. In truth, however, he is an angel dwelling among mortals; he lives a life of spiritual ecstasy that is exalted above all praise (*Kovetz Iggaros, Chazon Ish* 1:13).

◆§ Physical Forces — Lifeless Servants

Maharal of Prague (Nesivos Olam; Bitachon ch. 1) demonstrates how a person can live in *Olam Haba* while dwelling in this world. The key, he writes, is intense faith:

> The prophet cried out to Israel: *Place your trust in* HASHEM *forever and ever, for* HASHEM *is the sheltering Rock of both worlds (Isaiah* 26:4*)*. The Talmud (*Menachos* 29b) derives from this verse: The person who places his complete trust in Hashem will merit God as his Protection both in this world and in the World to Come.
>
> This means that even if one was originally destined to suffer in this world, the decree only remains as long as the person perceives himself to be under the control of physical forces. The God-fearing person, however, sees that the forces of nature are lifeless tools in the hands of a Creator who controls everything. This *bitachon* literally lifts the man of faith "out of this world"; he enters an entirely new sphere of existence, not unlike the World to Come. This God-fearing person appears to be no different than the masses of humanity, yet in reality he is entirely separated from them: He is surrounded by an other-worldly glow which shields him from the vicissitudes of mundane life.
>
> This is what King David meant when he sang: *You are shelter for me. From distress You preserve me. With glad song of rescue You envelope me, Selah! . . . Many are the agonies of the wicked — but he who trusts in* HASHEM, *kindness surrounds him (Psalms* 32:7,10).

◆§ A Parting Blessing

The Talmud (*Berachos* 17a) relates how the Sages would bless one another at the conclusion of their studies. They said: עוֹלָמְךָ תִּרְאֶה בְּחַיֶּיךָ וְאַחֲרִיתְךָ לְחַיֵּי עוֹלָם הַבָּא, *May you see your world in your lifetime, and may the conclusion of your life lead you on to the World to Come!* The meaning is this: "May you now apply the lessons you have just studied to your everyday life so that you will experience the bliss of the World to Come within your lifetime on earth. May this prepare you for your final reward when you will completely enter the World to Come."

14

וְעַתָּה בְּנִי דַע וּרְאֵה, כִּי הַמִּתְגָּאֶה בְּלִבּוֹ עַל הַבְּרִיּוֹת,
מוֹרֵד הוּא בְּמַלְכוּת שָׁמַיִם, כִּי מִתְפָּאֵר הוּא בִּלְבוּשׁ
מַלְכוּת שָׁמַיִם, שֶׁנֶּאֱמַר: ה' מָלָךְ גֵּאוּת לָבֵשׁ וְגוֹ'.

And now my son, understand clearly that one who is prideful in his heart towards other men rebels against the sovereignty of heaven, for he glorifies himself in God's own robes, for it is written, "HASHEM reigns, He dons the raiment of grandeur" *(Psalms 93:1).*

⋌§ The Faces of Pride

The Rebbe of Komarno in his work *Notzer Chessed* (*Avos* 4:4) observes that the proud person, insofar as he venerates himself, defies God by "worshiping" himself. The Talmud (*Avodah Zarah* 14b) teaches that Abraham composed a huge tractate concerning the prohibition against idol worship: It consisted of no less than four hundred chapters. The hundreds of chapters did not describe alien or pagan deities, but rather detailed the true source of idolatry: man's arrogance and pride.

Mesillas Yesharim (ch. 11) examines the many forms of arrogance in detail:

> Pride means that a person takes himself seriously — he feels that he is truly worthy of recognition and praise. There are many causes of these feelings. Some deem themselves intelli-

gent; some, handsome and distinguished. Others see themselves as great or wise. Proud men conduct themselves in a variety of ways in order to gain the recognition they so desperately crave.

One type of person adopts dignified mannerisms so as to make powerful impressions on others. He walks slowly, with a finely measured step; sits erect and rises only little by little, like a snake. He doesn't speak with just anybody — only with men of eminence and distinction. When he does talk, he does so in an enigmatic fashion designed to arouse wonder. In short, all of his movements are conducted with pompousness, as if his flesh were lead, and his bones, stone or earth.

Another type of proud person seeks to demonstrate his superiority by becoming an earthly terror. He agitates by speaking insolently, and drives men into frenzies with his biting retorts.

A third type of pride reveals itself in the man who thinks that he is already so invested with honor that honor is inseparable from him. To impress this upon others he imitates the conduct of the most humble men, while in truth his heart bursts with pride.

There are yet other types of pride which lay smoldering in the hearts of men ... concerning all forms of pride it is written: *The proud of heart are the abomination of HASHEM* (*Proverbs* 16:5).

✌§ A Tragic Consolation

It is especially important for those in the public eye to eradicate feelings of lordship. *Shulchan Aruch* (*Orach Chaim* 53:1) gives this admonition to the cantor who leads the congregation in prayer:

> He should stand before God in a solemn and reverent spirit, filled with trepidation and fear. If his purpose is to show his beautiful voice, and his heart rejoices in his cantorial skills — this is repulsive.

Mishnah Berurah (ibid. #35) comments: *Sefer Chassidim* records that when Rabban Shimon ben Gamliel was taken out to be killed [by the Romans], he turned to Rabbi Yishmael the High Priest and asked: "My dear brother, how have I sinned that I should merit such a terrible death?" Rabbi Yishmael replied: "Search your heart: Perhaps when you spoke publicly, at times you felt some pride in your heart, and thus you used words of Torah for your own delight." To this, Rabbi Shimon Ben Gamliel responds: "נִחַמְתָּנִי, You have consoled me for my death."

◆§ A Trace of Pride

When Rav Moshe Feinstein underwent difficult surgery to correct his pacemaker he tried to discover the sin that had caused his suffering. He was sure that his pain must be a punishment for having hurt someone else's feelings — but he could not recall having done so. He reviewed in his mind all the years of his life until he came to his childhood days. There, he found the source of his affliction. As a young *cheder* child he and a classmate had both offered an answer to their *rebbi's* question. Reb Moshe recalled feeling a sense of pride when the *rebbi* found his reasoning superior to that of his friend. While he had not actually done his friend any harm, still, he felt, it was wrong for him to feel uplifted by an incident that had embarrassed someone else. Reb Moshe viewed his mistake as an indirect form of מַלְבִּין פְּנֵי חֲבֵירוֹ, *shaming one's friend*, for which the surgery he was to undergo was a proper punishment.

15

וּבַמֶּה יִתְגָּאֶה לֵב הָאָדָם,
אִם בְּעוֹשֶׁר, ה' מוֹרִישׁ וּמַעֲשִׁיר.

For indeed, of what should man be prideful? If he has wealth — it is HASHEM who makes one prosperous.

⋙ The Illusion of Power

> Fear not when a man grows rich, when he increases the splendor of his house. For upon his death he will not take anything, his splendor will not descend after him (Psalms 49:17-18).

While wealth can be a blessing from God, if it is not realized as such, it can also become a source of undue pride. One of the most tragic examples of a man whose heart grew proud as a result of fabulous riches was Korach; his arrogance ultimately led him to challenge the authority of Moshe Rabbeinu himself. When Korach was swallowed into the earth as punishment, it was fitting that his vast possessions perished with him. The Midrash says that even Korach's clothes and those of his followers, even their names which were inscribed on legal documents, even the tiny sewing needles which they had loaned to others, all were swallowed whole by the earth (*Midrash Bamidbar Rabbah* 18:13; *Jerusalem Talmud Sanhedrin* 10:1). In obliterating the last vestiges of Korach's wealth, God demonstrated that man never becomes omnipotent, despite his accumulation of all things material.

⋖§ The Downfall of Nakdimon

Wealth is indeed a tool which must be used properly. The Talmud writes that God judges one not only by the acts of charity one performs, but by his intentions in performing them as well.

The Talmud tells that the Sages once chanced upon the daughter of Nakdimon ben Gurion, a man of immense wealth. To their astonishment, they found her scrounging in the dung of animals belonging to Arabs, searching for kernels of barley to satiate her hunger. So tattered were her garments that she had wrapped herself in her long, wild tresses of hair. Her wedding dowry had been one million golden zuzim. The Sages were astonished at her tragic descent into poverty.

She explained the cause of the terrible reverse in her family's fortunes: "The people of Jerusalem have a saying for it, מֶלַח מָמוֹן חָסֵר, *the salt* (preservative) *of money is depletion* (expenditure for charity) (*Kesubos* 66b-67a) — by not giving generously, we have doomed ourselves to this tragic fate."

The Talmud is puzzled: Was not Nakdimon known for his acts of great charity? The Talmud concludes that: 'The charity which Nakdimon performed, was solely for the purpose of enhancing his own honor.'

Yad Yoseif (comm. to *Psalms* 49:17-18, see *ArtScroll Tehillim*) writes that the Psalmist alludes to the tragic fate of Nakdimon and his likes: *Fear not when a man grows rich ... for upon his death he will not take anything ...* When a man misuses his wealth, it will ultimately be lost. When his charity is used to *increase the splendor of his house*, then indeed, *his splendor will not descend after him —* even his acts of charity will not rescue him from an ignoble fate.

⋖§ The Masquerade of Rags

Elsewhere, Talmud demonstrates that the wealth and status which men enjoy in this world can sometimes be illusory:

> The son of Rabbi Yehoshua ben Levi was desperately ill. While in a deep coma, he had a vision of the World to Come. When he regained consciousness, his father asked him, "My son — what did you see in your vision?" The son responded, "I saw a world where everything was upside down. In the world of the future, the powerful men, who are on top here,

are on the bottom; while those who are humble in this world are on top there — enjoying the highest distinction." Rabbi Yehoshua ben Levi answered: "My son, the world which you saw was not upside down at all; it was actually perfectly in order" (*Bava Basra* 10a).

The Chofetz Chaim (*Shem Olam*, part II, ch. 9) offers insights into the story: The vision which the son saw, explained R' Yehoshua, was not the World to Come at all — it was merely a proper vision of this world. Although God allows men to carry themselves pompously on this earth, their success is only a facade. In truth, they have *already* sunk into bankruptcy, for the arrogant have already consumed their Heavenly reward within their lifetimes. The humble who appear downtrodden in this world are the truly wealthy people: Their graceful and dignified struggle has already increased their spiritual stature; their heavenly portion remains intact and undiminished. It is only the mortal eye which fails to perceive that the rags of the humble poor are the clothes of a masquerade.

16

וְאִם בְּכָבוֹד, הֲלֹא לֵאלֹקִים הוּא, שֶׁנֶּאֱמַר: וְהָעוֹשֶׁר
וְהַכָּבוֹד מִלְּפָנֶיךָ, וְאֵיךְ מִתְפָּאֵר בִּכְבוֹד קוֹנוֹ.

If it is honor — does not honor belong to God? As it is written: Wealth and honor come from You *(I Chronicles 29:12)* **— how can one glorify himself with the honor of his Maker?**

✎§ *The Most Coveted of Delights*

Mesillas Yesharim (ch. 11) posits that it is the pursuit of glory which is man's essential drive. More than money, power, or physical pleasure, man yearns for honor.

Ramban here hints at how we may understand this: God has bestowed upon mankind every resource for attaining pleasure on earth. Honor, however, He has left as a lone exception. People can "purchase" external, insincere honor, but true honor, the most coveted of delights, remains in the possession of God Himself. Alas, it is human nature to yearn for the inaccessible — thus, ultimate honor is all the more sought after by mortals.

✎§ *Attributing Honor to Its Source*

The Talmud (*Chullin* 89a) records that an outstanding innate quality of the Jew is that when he is commended, he reacts with humility, attributing glory to God:

> The Holy One, Blessed is He, said to Israel: "My sons! I yearn for you because even when I shower glory upon you, you make

little of yourselves in deference to Me. I gave great glory to Abraham and he said: *I am naught but dust and ashes (Genesis* 18:27). I bestowed greatness upon Moses and Aaron and they said: *What are we? (Exodus* 16:7). I elevated David to lofty heights and he said: *And I am a worm and not a man (Psalms* 22:7). But when I lifted the gentile rulers to glory — Nimrod, Pharaoh, Sennacherib and Nebuchadnezzar — they waxed proud and reacted with blasphemous arrogance."

~§ Arrogance: The Eclipse of Heavenly Glory

Mesillas Yesharim (ch. 22) writes that an honest man realizes that his accomplishments are a barometer of his obligations:

Rabbi Yisrael Salanter used to say: "I know that in many ways I have the capacity of one thousand men; but because of this, my obligation to serve Hashem is also that of one thousand men."

One who attributes undue honor to himself not only engages in an act of distasteful vanity; *Ramban* writes that he literally detracts from the honor due to God Himself. As King Solomon said: תּוֹעֲבַת ה' כָּל גְּבַהּ לֵב יָד יָד לֹא יִנָּקֶה, *All proud of heart are the abomination of HASHEM; hand to hand he shall not go unpunished (Proverbs* 16:5). *Malbim* explains that although God is patient with transgressors, He punishes the arrogant immediately and directly, *hand to hand*. Indeed, it is man's arrogance that vaingloriously eclipses the splendor of his Creator.

~§ The Idol of One's Own Likeness

God created the world so that He be recognized by mankind — and mankind, so that they recognize their Creator. To the extent that man magnifies himself, he thus detracts from his purpose of existence. Hence, God declares, "He [the arrogant man] and I cannot exist in the same world" (*Sotah* 5a). In venerating himself, the arrogant man worships the idol of his own likeness.

~§ The Responsibility of Authority

The *Chofetz Chaim* writes that power buries those who improperly wield it. Although a father deserves his son's recognition, he ought not place too heavy a burden on his son, nor treat him callously. If one is elevated to a position of authority, he must take care to treat those beneath him with consideration. Our Sages taught that Joseph, who was next to the youngest of his brothers died before all of them because he lorded over them. It is the task of a leader to remain aware that power buries those who improperly wield it (*Machaneh Yisrael* II:3).

17

וְאִם מִתְפָּאֵר בְּחָכְמָה, מֵסִיר שָׂפָה לְנֶאֱמָנִים,
וְטַעַם זְקֵנִים יִקָּח.

If he takes pride in wisdom — let him understand that God may remove the speech of the most competent and take away the wisdom of the aged *(Job 12:20).*

◆§ Humility — The Mark of Scholarship

The Talmud (*Shabbos* 152a) teaches:

> As Torah scholars age, their wisdom increases; as ignorant men grow old, their ignorance increases, as it says: *He removes the speech of the most competent, and takes away the wisdom of the aged.*

In alluding to this Talmudic passage, *Ramban* implies that the haughty person who prides himself as a Torah scholar entertains a distorted perception of Torah. Genuine Torah scholarship makes one humble, not proud. When one studies properly, the more he learns the more he is overwhelmed by how little he knows. Thus, the one who grows haughty from his studies attests to the superficiality of his knowledge.

◆§ A Product of Nature

Intelligent thought is man's supreme faculty. Yet, although wisdom is laudable, it may at the same time provoke feelings of self-importance. *Mesillas Yesharim* (ch. 22) warns:

First of all, even the finest mind is imperfect and prone to error. Even the most accomplished sage makes mistakes. Secondly, a person really deserves little credit for his genius; the man who knows more than others merely follows the dictates of his nature and is no different than the bird whose nature is to flap its wings and fly ... One is wise only because his nature has led him to be so ... There is no room for pride in respect to wisdom: Rather, if one has acquired knowledge, he is duty bound to share it with others who are in need of it. As Rabban Yochanan ben Zakkai states in *Mishnah Avos* (2:9): "If you have learned much Torah, do not take credit for yourself, for it was for this purpose that you were created."

◆§ The Silent Discourse

When the righteous men of Simunya implored Rabbi Judah the Prince to send one of his choice disciples to be their rav, R' Judah recommended Rabbi Levi bar Sisai (known in the Talmud simply as "Levi"), a profound scholar and a brilliant orator. When the new rav arrived in Simunya, the people showered him with honor and placed him on a platform from which he would deliver his first Torah discourse. However, when R' Levi opened his mouth to speak, no words came forth — his mind registered a blank. The people attempted to break the agonizing silence by asking him questions, but the new rabbi did not respond. Humiliated, R' Levi descended the dais and returned to R' Judah.

When he completed his journey home, his brilliance and wisdom returned. "So what happened in Simunya?" asked Rabbi Judah the Prince.

R' Levi replied, "Rebbi, I now realized that when I stood on that platform I felt a surge of pride in my heart and that erased all the Torah from my mind."

Rabbi Judah exclaimed, "Your experience is vivid proof of the verse in *Proverbs* (30:32): *If you were utterly degraded, it is because you were lifted too high!*" (*Yalkut Shimoni, Mishlei* #964).

◆§ The Elegance of Humility

A certain Jewish tailor living near Pshis'chah was commissioned by the local squire (*paritz*) to create a cloak from a bolt of expensive fabric purchased in Paris. The nobleman warned the tailor to take pains to create a masterpiece.

The tailor laughed and protested: "Sire, why do you say such a thing? Am I not known to be the most expert tailor in the entire province?"

When the tailor presented the finished garment to the *paritz*, the upperclassman was dissatisfied. The squire abused the tailor, claiming he had ruined the precious fabric, and threw him out of his home. In desperation, the tailor sought out the counsel of Reb Yerachmiel, the son of the *Yid HaKadosh* of Pshis'chah. The Sage advised, "Undo all the stitches in the garment, and sew it back together in exactly the same pattern as before. Then bring the cloak back to the *paritz*."

The tailor did so, and brought the reconstituted garment back to the squire for whom he sewed it. To the tailor's surprise, the squire exclaimed his delight with the finished product. He sang the tailor's praises and added a bonus to his fee.

Mystified by this turn of events, the tailor returned to the *tzaddik*. Gently, R' Yerachmiel explained: "Originally when you showed me your handiwork I could tell that when you first made the cloak you made it out of arrogance — and arrogance has no grace. That's why the *paritz* rejected your work. But this very rebuff made you humble and broken hearted. That's why I told you to undo the arrogant stitches and to sew the cloak anew — in humility. Thus the cloak acquired grace and elegance, and your prestige grew in the eyes of the *paritz*."

18

נִמְצָא הַכֹּל שָׁוֶה לִפְנֵי הַמָּקוֹם,
כִּי בְאַפּוֹ מַשְׁפִּיל גֵּאִים, וּבִרְצוֹנוֹ מַגְבִּיהַ שְׁפָלִים,
לָכֵן הַשְׁפִּיל עַצְמְךָ וְיִנְשַׂאֲךָ הַמָּקוֹם.

Thus, all men stand as equals before their Creator. In His fury He casts down the lofty; in His goodwill He elevates the downtrodden. Therefore, humble yourself, for HASHEM will lift you.

◆§ The Frailty of Fortune

Ramban's words are based on the song of Chanah, the mother of Samuel the prophet: ה' מוֹרִישׁ וּמַעֲשִׁיר מַשְׁפִּיל אַף מְרוֹמֵם, *HASHEM impoverishes and makes prosperous, He lowers and He uplifts (I Samuel 2:7).* Similarly, in *Psalms 75:8* we read: אֱלֹהִים שֹׁפֵט זֶה יַשְׁפִּיל וְזֶה יָרִים, *God is the Judge, He lowers one and raises another.*

The Midrash (*Shemos Rabbah* 31:14) states:

> This world may be likened to a water wheel which irrigates a field. It scoops water from a stream below and lifts the water to the elevated field. Then it descends again, empty. Men's fortunes rise and fall in a similar manner.

Another Midrash (*Bamidbar Rabbah* 22:7-8) writes that a noblewoman once asked Rabbi Shimon ben Chalafta, "What has God been doing since the six days of Creation?" The Sage replied, "Since that time until this very day, God has been making ladders upon which He lowers one man while He raises another."

In this vein the Midrash (ibid.) explains: Property is called נְכָסִים, for possessions נִכְסִים, vanish, from the hands of one owner and reappear in the hands of another. Similarly, coins are called זוּזִים: They are constantly זָזִים, moving away, from one man to another. Funds are called מָמוֹן, for we may ask their possessor, "Why do you bother to מוֹנֶה, count, the money? Soon it shall be gone." Pieces of currency are מָעוֹת: for we may wonder: מַה לְעֵת, "What is the value of something which lasts only a short time?"

◄§ Halachah Follows Beis Hillel

Ramban urges: "Humble yourself and HASHEM will elevate you." The advice is amplified by the Talmud (Eruvin 13b) which observes that in numerous halachic disputes between Beis Hillel and Beis Shammai, the halachah is decided in accordance with the opinion of Beis Hillel. The reason given does not revolve around the intellectual prowess of Beis Hillel, but rather around their character:

> Beis Hillel merited to have the halachah determined according to their opinion because the members of Hillel's Academy were mild mannered, soft spoken and patient. Furthermore, whenever Beis Hillel spoke, they would cite the opinions and arguments of Beis Shammai before citing their own. This teaches that whoever humbles himself merits that the Holy One, Blessed is He, will Himself raise him up.

◄§ Joseph's Reward

Although the humble man does not seek fame, by virtue of his humility he sometimes attains a measure of glory:

In his youth Joseph displayed an ambition tinged with the subtleties of pride. The years of imprisonment and suffering in Egypt, however, imbued Joseph with a deep sense of humility. When Pharaoh marveled at his ability to interpret dreams, Joseph refused to take credit. He proclaimed, בִּלְעָדָי אֱלֹהִים יַעֲנֶה אֶת שְׁלוֹם פַּרְעֹה, It is not I! It is God who responds with Pharaoh's well-being (Genesis 41:16).

Said the Holy One, Blessed is He: "You, Joseph, refused to elevate yourself; I promise you that in the merit of your humility I will raise you to greatness" (Midrash Tanchuma).

In his youth, Shneur Zalman of Liadi, destined to become the great *Baal HaTanya*, studied under the tutelage of Reb Dov Ber, the Maggid of Mezritch. Late one night young Zalman knocked on his Rebbe's door to ask him a difficult Talmudic question. The Rebbe called out, "Who's there?" The youngster responded, "It's me!" confident that he would be recognized. The Rebbe repeated his query, "Who's there?" and again the reply came, "It's me!" Yet a third time the Rebbe cried out, "Who's there?" Finally the young student answered his name. "Zalman," he said. The Rebbe opened the door and said, "My dear Zalman, the time has come for *uprichten golus* — a self-imposed exile. You will travel incognito to faraway places. When you return, we will analyze your experiences together."

In the course of his wanderings Shneur Zalman chanced upon a roadside inn, where he took lodging for the night. That same evening, thieves broke in and stole the inn's silverware. The next morning the innkeeper's suspicious gaze fell upon the young stranger, Zalman.

"Come on," snarled the innkeeper, "confess that it was you who stole my silver!"

"It was not me! Not me!" Zalman cried back. But the innkeeper took him in his grasp, and intensified his vicious accusations. "Not me! Not me!" yelled Zalman repeatedly. Finally the youngster tore himself from the innkeeper's grip and fled back to Mezritch.

After the holy Maggid heard this tale from his student, he observed: "This, my dear Zalman, is a lesson which you should never forget. Do you see how many times you were forced to shout, "Not me! Not me!" in order to undo the effect of calling out proudly, "It's me"?

19

וְרֹאשְׁךָ כָּפוּף, וְעֵינֶיךָ יַבִּיטוּ לְמַטָּה לָאָרֶץ,
וְלִבְּךָ לְמַעְלָה.

Let your head be bowed. Cast your eyes downward, and your heart heavenward.

This statement has its origins in *Yevamos* 105b:

> When praying, one should train his eyes downward — as it is written: *My eyes and my heart shall be there all the time* (*I Kings* 9:3). Likewise, he should focus his heart heavenward, as it is written: *Let us lift our hearts with our hands to God in heaven* (*Lamentations* 3:41).

◆§ Frailty and Grandeur: The Two Eyes of Man

When the prayer experience truly becomes an encounter with God, the supplicant finds himself gripped by contradictory emotions. On the one hand, the mortal who stands before the King of kings is overwhelmed by awe. As he confronts the unutterable majesty of his Creator, he has no choice but to recoil in trepidation. Simultaneously however, a different feeling begins to swell in his heart. As the worshiper intuits the almost tangible closeness of his Heavenly Father, he is overcome by a sense of boundless love. His heart leaps for joy, thrilled at the opportunity to communicate directly and personally with the Eternal Master of the universe. To pray effectively, the worshiper must strike a delicate balance between these opposing emotions and moods, blending the two in a state of mental harmony.

In reflecting upon this dichotomy, Rav Yisrael, the Kozhnitzer Maggid, allegorically explained why God chose to create man with two eyes: to symbolize that man ought to have two sorts of vision. With one eye he looks upward, and with the other he gazes downward. In contemporary terms, with one eye man's vision lacks depth and perspective. With it, he would gaze at the cosmos around him, feeling dwarfed by its vastness. He may stare into the mirror of his likeness, recognizing his own frailty. With the other eye, though, man gains perspective. He perceives the presence of the Almighty, and is inspired to stand erect. Although he can see with only one, he needs both of his eyes to fully understand the truth of his surroundings (see *Avodas Yisrael, Parashas Mishpatim*).

~§ Approaching the Celestial Throne

In his commentary to *Berachos* (ch. 5), *Rabbeinu Yonah* describes the process of developing a proper mental state for prayer. His advice is based upon the same excerpt of Talmud referred to above by the *Ramban*:

> When a person prays, he must visualize himself as standing before God's Celestial Throne. This is impossible as long as he is weighed down by mundane affairs — financial worries, business problems and the like. Therefore, before praying, he must first look downward to discard all earthly concerns. Earlier generations had a saying for this: כְּשֶׁתִּרְצֶה לְכַוֵּון פְּשׁוֹט גּוּפְךָ מֵעַל נִשְׁמָתְךְ, *If you wish to concentrate on your prayers, first you must strip your soul of your body*. Only then can your heart be released to alight heavenward!

~§ The Statement of Posture

One's mannerisms reflect, and to a certain extent determine, his more deeply hidden emotions and thoughts. The Talmud (*Kiddushin* 31a) teaches that it is prohibited to walk four cubits with an upright posture which displays arrogance. The Talmud cites the verse מְלֹא כָל הָאָרֶץ כְּבוֹדוֹ, *The entire world is filled with God's glory* (Isaiah 6:3), as the source of its ruling. Likewise, *Rambam* (*Hilchos De'os* 5:8) writes that men of true stature, as a rule, refrain from walking completely erect; rather, "a wise person should always cast his gaze downward like a person standing in prayer."

An erect posture, however, is only the external indication of internal feelings. The tone of man's relationship with God is determined, more than anything else, by his heart: It is indeed possible for one to stand ramrod straight and yet assume an internal posture of surrender to his Creator's will.

It was the practice of HaRav Moshe Feinstein to stand motionless and perfectly erect while reciting the *Shemoneh Esrei*, except when required to bow. In explanation, he once related that when Russian Communists held him for interrogation concerning his involvement in religious activities, he had been forced to stand rigidly at attention, while a menacing guard stood watch. Never, Rav Moshe related, had he felt so subservient. It was at that point that he decided that from this unflinching position he would recite *Shemoneh Esrei* and demonstrate his subservience to the true Ruler.

◆§ The Significance of Dust

Throughout the generations, holy men have found it helpful to keep their eyes trained downward. *Reishis Chachmah* (*Shaar Hakedushah*, ch. 8, #18) writes:

> When a person stares down at the earth he reminds himself that he is, after all, nothing more than dust, and that he shall return to dust. In this way he will not be seduced to pursue the fleeting desires of this world.

Pela Yoetz (*Reish*) explains that one weakens his desire for material things by looking at the dust, the meager basis of all things physical. To the extent that one thereby increases his striving for the world of the spiritual, the author adds, will one's prayers truly be answered, as it says: וְשַׁח עֵינַיִם יוֹשִׁעַ, *He who casts his eyes downward will be saved* (Job 22:29).

20

וְאַל תַּבִּיט בִּפְנֵי אָדָם בְּדַבֶּרְךָ עִמּוֹ,
וְכָל אָדָם יִהְיֶה גָּדוֹל מִמְּךָ בְּעֵינֶיךָ.

Do not stare at your listener [to intimidate or belittle him]. Let all men seem greater than you in your eyes.

◄§ Subtle Barbs

Throughout his letter, *Ramban* points out various manifestations of arrogance. Here he notes the habit of the overbearing individual to lord over others in ways that are often quite subtle. Arrogance intimidates, no matter what its form. One need not verbally assault another in order to hurt him; the penetrating coldness of a quick glance can be just as painful a message. Indeed, one must strive to refine *all* aspects of his communication with others.

◄§ The Deciding Matchstick

The great teachers of the Mussar movement used a parable to illustrate the psychology of the overbearing individual.
Imagine the following scenario:

> One day the two richest men in the world happened to meet. They conversed, and eventually came to discuss the immensity of their respective assets. Each was eager to establish himself as the wealthier, and they began to list to one another their entire holdings. As the hours went by, they found to their amazement that their fortunes were exactly equal. Neck to neck, the contest

continued, until there was nothing left to count. Exasperated, one of the men withdrew a small case from his pocket: "Seventeen matches!" he called out. The other reached into his pocket and laid out tiny sticks upon the table. Slowly he counted: ". . . sixteen, seventeen . . . eighteen. Eighteen matches. Ah! I am the richest man, the richest in the world. And you — you are nothing but a wretched pauper."

Every person is created in God's image. Every person, in his very existence, possesses unimaginable wealth. The physical and intellectual gifts of a mere child are uncountable. What then, are one man's advantages over another? A hint of talent, a shade of beauty sink into meaninglessness when seen in perspective of the common pricelessness of the human being. He who looks down upon others betrays his inability to grasp man's true greatness.

◆§ Let all men seem greater than you in your eyes

A popular folktale runs as follows:

Once there was a man who imagined himself to be a true *talmid chacham*. He arose at 4:00 a.m. every morning to study in the *Beis HaMidrash*. On his way he would always meet a poor and ignorant shoemaker who also would rise early to eke out his meager livelihood. As the two passed one another, the former's heart was filled with pride over his scholarship and diligence while he looked down upon the ignorant shoemaker with utter contempt. When the shoemaker saw the man he passed on his daily journey, however, he felt deep respect for his scholarship. This daily encounter went on for years and years.

Finally, the time came for both men to leave this world to stand in final judgment. The contempt which the arrogant scholar felt for the shoemaker outweighed his good deeds and tipped the scales against him. All of the shoemaker's errors and shortcomings, however, were balanced by the one sigh of humility which he would sigh every morning when he looked up to the *talmid chacham*. In its merit the humble shoemaker entered *Gan Eden*.

It is the man who seems smugly self assured who views every human being as a potential threat; a possible competitor in the never-ending race for approval. Lacking the resources to trust his own self image, he is enslaved to other's opinions of him. It is by denigrating his fellow, that the arrogant man gains the illusion of relative strength.

21

וְאִם חָכָם אוֹ עָשִׁיר הוּא, עָלֶיךָ לְכַבְּדוֹ.

If another is more wise or wealthy than yourself, you must show him respect.

◆§ The Sanctity of Knowledge

מִפְּנֵי שֵׂיבָה תָּקוּם וְהָדַרְתָּ פְּנֵי זָקֵן וְיָרֵאתָ מֵאֱלֹהֶיךָ, *Arise respectfully before the elderly, honor the presence of the scholar, and be in fear of your God* (*Leviticus* 19:32).

Man is influenced by his actions. When one shows outward signs of respect to the wise, he becomes inspired to emulate their example (*Sefer HaChinuch* #257). Citing the great scholar Rabbi Abba HaCohen, the Midrash relates:

> Originally I would avoid walking past crowds of people so as not to bother them, for I knew that they would stand as I walked by. But Rabbi Yossi advised me otherwise: When crowds rise before a Torah scholar, their hearts become filled with the fear of Heaven.

Conversely, failure to show outward deference to scholars is indicative of an inner lack of regard for the sanctity of knowledge. A scholar, who does not show respect for his peers, thus lives a life of contradiction — his knowledge suffers from a tragic flaw:

> Rabbi Eliezer said: "Any Torah student who fails to stand up respectfully for his Rabbi and teacher is called wicked ... He is destined to forget his Torah knowledge" (*Kiddushin* 33b).

⊷§ The Gift of Prosperity: Blessing and Toxin

Besides demanding that he show deference to the wise, *Ramban* also encourages his son to respect men of wealth. Indeed, the Rabbis teach that when one acknowledges that his riches are a gift from God, his wealth becomes a true Divine blessing. It is only when one sees his gain as solely the product of his own industry that affluence becomes laced with spiritual toxin (*Midrash Bamidbar Rabbah* 22:6).

Ultimately, it is essential that one realize the value of the resources he is equipped with. Both wisdom and money are reservoirs of spiritual potential. Rabbi Yechiel HaRofeh, in an essay on the value of wealth (in his work *Maalos HaMiddos*), writes that a sage was once asked: "Why do we often see wise men seeking out the company of the wealthy, but seldom do we see wealthy men seeking out the presence of the wise?" The sage replied, "that is because wise men appreciate the true value of wealth, whereas wealthy men fail to appreciate the value of wisdom."

⊷§ The Bounds of Humility

רַבִּי מְכַבֵּד עֲשִׁירִים, רַבִּי עֲקִיבָא מְכַבֵּד עֲשִׁירִים, *Rabbi Judah the Prince and Rabbi Akiva gave recognition to the rich* (Eruvin 86a).

The Talmud (ibid., 85b) relates how a young man named Bunyas ben Bunyas once came to the *yeshivah* of Rabbi Judah the Prince. He was clothed modestly, and received no special attention. As time passed, Rabbi Judah was informed that the young man's father possessed fabulous wealth, owning title to whole cities. Rabbi Judah responded, "In that case, please communicate to Bunyas the elder that he has failed to dress his son properly. A rich man's clothing should be an accurate reflection of his wealth."

The fantastically wealthy man — no less than anyone else — must not deny his uniqueness. Although modesty is laudable, one may not utilize humility as a vehicle for neglecting his primary mission in life. Just as the scholar, in his humility, may not avoid his duty to teach and define questions of Torah law, so too humility is inappropriate for the rich man if he is thus led to deny his role as a financial backbone of Jewish society.

⊷§ The Threads of Destiny

Look around you in the great house of your [Heavenly] Father . . . Everything sustains and is sustained, everything takes and gives and receives a thousandfold in giving — for it receives life instead of mere existence. And do you alone wish only to take and not to give? ... Would you be as a stream which dries up in the arid sand and fails to give back to the sea that which it has received? Once you have pondered upon the thought — that you are nothing so long as you exist only for yourself, that you only become something when you mean something to others; ... that you only possess something when you share it with others — that even the penny in your pocket is not yours but only becomes so when you spend it for a blessed purpose; then will you rejoice in the great task to which God has called you ... (R' S. R. Hirsch, *Horeb*, p. 427).

A first step in spiritual growth is identifying the unique tools of one's life mission. A man's spiritual potential is often a puzzle, the key to which may often seem unlikely — it is not always easy to distinguish the threads of destiny. Rabbi Akiva told Turnus Rufus, the Roman Governor of Judea, that an individual's state of poverty is not an indication of personal unworthiness; rather, it may be a Divine tool to enable the rich to help others (*Bava Basra* 10a). Truly, when one in the end unravels for himself his spiritual assets, he need not be ashamed of them. Both the poor and the rich have cause to humbly rejoice in their charge.

✺§ To Honor All Men

A sage was once asked: "How come you are accepted as the undisputed leader of the people of your generation?" He replied: "I have never met any person in whom I did not detect some quality in which he was superior to me. If he was wiser than I, I suspected that he might also be more God fearing. If he was less wise, I considered that on the Day of Judgment he will be held less accountable than I — for my transgressions were committed with full knowledge, while his were committed in error. If he was older, I would reason that the merits which he already acquired must exceed mine. If he was younger, I calculated that his sins were fewer than mine ... If the man was richer, then perhaps his wealth has enabled him to surpass me in serving God. If he was poorer, I would consider him to be contrite and of a humbler spirit than I. Thus, I honored all men and humbled myself before them" (*Chovos HaLevovos, Shaar HaKeniah*, ch. 10).

22

וְאִם רָשׁ הוּא, וְאַתָּה עָשִׁיר אוֹ חָכָם מִמֶּנּוּ,
חֲשׁוֹב בְּלִבְּךָ כִּי אַתָּה חַיָּב מִמֶּנּוּ וְהוּא זַכַּאי מִמְּךָ,
שֶׁאִם הוּא חוֹטֵא הוּא שׁוֹגֵג וְאַתָּה מֵזִיד.

**And if he is poor, and you are richer or
wiser than he, consider that he may be
more righteous than yourself:
If he sins it is the result of error,
while your transgression is deliberate.**

✑ Rav Chiya's Counsel

The Talmud (*Shabbos* 151b) relates that Rabbi Chiya told his wife:
"When you see a beggar approaching the door, don't wait for him to
knock — rather run out and offer food to him. In this merit, perhaps if
our children must ever beg, they will be treated in the same respectful
and considerate fashion." She responded, "Are you then cursing our
children that they be beggars?" "No," Rabbi Chiya replied, "but it is
inevitable that some form of poverty visit every family in the course of
its history: גַּלְגַּל הוּא שֶׁחוֹזֵר בָּעוֹלָם, *it is a wheel that rotates through the
world.*"

If one sees his wealth as tenuous, he equips himself to maintain
perspective upon his life.

✑ Subtle Shades of Charity

Pela Yoetz (מערכת כבוד הבריות) cites a Midrash which states that one
must stand when a poor man passes by, in acknowledgment that the

Almighty Himself accompanies the steps of the poor. As the Psalmist says: כִּי יַעֲמֹד לִימִין אֶבְיוֹן, *For He stands at the right side of the destitute* (*Psalms* 109:31). Similarly, the author writes that one should carefully avoid even subtle discrimination against men of lesser means. In personal celebrations, he advises, one should avoid allowing seating arrangements to reflect class distinctions.

R' Moshe Feinstein was especially attuned to the psychological effects of his actions in his dealings with the poverty stricken:

> A car pulled up in front of Mesivtha Tifereth Jerusalem to take the *Rosh HaYeshivah*, Rav Moshe Feinstein, to an important meeting. There was no time for delay. As Rav Moshe was about to get into the car, a poor man asked him for charity. Rav Moshe gave him some money, but the beggar persisted in speaking to the *Rosh HaYeshivah*. As the man drew out the conversation, the waiting driver became more and more impatient. A few students attempted to tell the pauper that Rav Moshe was in a great hurry. The sage signaled for them to go away. After ten minutes, Rav Moshe excused himself, shook hands with the beggar and finally got into the car.
>
> Rav Moshe explained to the driver and to his students: "You must understand that to this man the conversation meant more than the money. My *mitzvah* of *tzedakah* included showing him that I care about what he thinks and that I am not too busy to speak to him."

◈§ Sensing the Dignity of Humanity

Through his conduct, Rav Moshe Feinstein taught that the mentally ill must also be treated with dignity. One day, his *shiur* in Mesiftha Tifereth Jerusalem was interrupted by a man who sat reviewing the *sidrah* in a loud voice. A student went over to the man and told him that he was disturbing the *Rosh HaYeshivah's shiur*. However, the man, seemingly oblivious to what he had just been told, continued his chanting just as before. Several students then suggested to Reb Moshe that they escort the man out of the *beis midrash*. "No," came the reply. "He doesn't know what he's doing. I will speak louder." And so the *shiur* continued, with Reb Moshe speaking as loud as he could, while the man went on with his chanting, undisturbed.

Indeed, Reb Moshe also taught that it is not only Jews whom one must respect. There was an old Russian who worked as a janitor in

Mesiftha Tifereth Jerusalem. He spoke little English and few paid much attention to him. One day he suffered from a toothache and walked around with a kerchief tied around his cheeks. When Reb Moshe met the janitor in the hallway he stopped and spoke to him in Russian for a few minutes. When the conversation ended, the janitor walked away happier than anyone could ever remember seeing him.

৺§ A Military Secret

Rav Eliyahu Moshe Shisgal, Rav Moshe's son-in-law, followed his father-in-law's example of treating all of God's creations with respect. Rav Shisgal befriended a mentally ill person who imagined himself to be both a medical genius and a high-ranking army official. The odd Jew enjoyed being addressed as "The Professor."

Once Rav Shisgal invited The Professor to his home.

The Professor had brought along a transistor radio, which he proudly showed off. He turned the radio to its highest volume and proceeded to switch from station to station — over and over again. The Professor, who was evidently enjoying himself immensely, assumed that others enjoyed this as well. Rav Shisgal did not have the heart to dampen the man's spirits by asking him to turn off the radio.

Suddenly, Rav Shisgal had an idea. He put his ear to the radio and said, "Professor, are these military secrets that I hear?"

"Yes," the Professor shouted excitedly. "This is a military radio and it carries military secrets!"

"Well," said Rav Shisgal, "as you know I am not a member of the military. I probably should not be hearing these things."

"You are right," the Professor replied, and promptly turned off the radio.

৺§ A Puzzling Departure

"Consider that he may be more righteous than yourself . . ."

By honoring all men, despite their outward status, one fulfills the mitzvah of בְּצֶדֶק תִּשְׁפֹּט עֲמִיתֶךָ, *You shall judge your fellow man with fairness* (*Leviticus* 19:15).

Rabbi Aryeh Levin of Jerusalem excelled in his ability to see no evil in his fellow Jew. He once related that the following incident helped him to adopt this quality.

Once Reb Aryeh attended the funeral of a certain Reb Eliezer, a man who had been an honest and compassionate distributor of charity funds.

A man named Reb Shmuel, the deceased Reb Eliezer's best friend for over thirty years, also participated in the funeral procession. As Reb Aryeh watched in astonishment, Reb Shmuel abruptly left the funeral cortege to enter a flower shop. Moments later, the man emerged, and continued walking along with the burial procession, but carrying a clay pot.

Reb Aryeh was deeply disturbed by this apparently callous behavior. Later that day, he reproached Reb Shmuel for abandoning his best friend's funeral.

Reb Shmuel explained: "For years I have been visiting a Jew stricken with leprosy. Yesterday he died. The doctors at the sanitarium — who are non-Jews — fear for contagion, so they ordered that all the leper's clothing and possessions be burned — including the man's pair of *Tefillin*. After I pleaded with one of the doctors, he agreed to spare the *Tefillin* if I could arrange to have them safely buried before noon today. In order to satisfy both medical and halachic requirements, I needed an earthenware container. It was because of this that I was compelled to leave the funeral to buy the flowerpot."

"Since that incident," said Reb Aryeh Levin, "I firmly resolved to judge every person favorably."

23

בְּכָל דְּבָרֶיךָ וּמַעֲשֶׂיךָ וּמַחְשְׁבוֹתֶיךָ וּבְכָל עֵת,
חֲשׁוֹב בְּלִבְּךָ כְּאִלּוּ אַתָּה עוֹמֵד לִפְנֵי הקב"ה,
וּשְׁכִינָתוֹ עָלֶיךָ. כִּי כְּבוֹדוֹ מָלֵא הָעוֹלָם,
וּדְבָרֶיךָ יִהְיוּ בְּאֵימָה וּבְיִרְאָה כְּעֶבֶד לִפְנֵי רַבּוֹ.

In all your words, actions and thoughts — at all times — imagine in your heart that you are standing in the presence of the Holy One, Blessed is He, and that His Presence rests upon you . . . Act with restraint in the company of others: If one should call out to you, do not answer with a loud voice, but respond gently — in low tones, as one who stands before his mentor.

◈§ *The Keys of Restraint*

Recognition of God's presence inspires man to lead a life style balanced with restraint. *Rav Moshe Isserles* writes the following in his introduction to the *Shulchan Aruch*:

> שִׁוִּיתִי ה' לְנֶגְדִּי תָמִיד, *I have set HASHEM before me at all times* (*Psalms* 16:8). This principle is the fundamental theme underlying Torah observance and all the lofty accomplishments of the righteous.

We do not sit, move or conduct ourselves when we are at home the same way as we would in the presence of a king. Although we speak as we please when we are with our relatives, we don't act as freely when we are in royal audience. All the more so then, should we be careful when we take to heart that we are constantly in the presence of the mightiest of kings, the Holy One, Blessed is He ... He carefully observes our every action, as it is written: *Can any man hide himself in secret places so that I shall not see him? says* HASHEM (*Jeremiah* 23:24).

The ability to feel ashamed of one's actions also indicates the degree to which one feels responsible for them. The Talmud writes:

> Whomsoever is bashful will not easily come to sin, but whoever has no shame proves that his forebears did not stand at Mount Sinai (*Yevamos* 79a).

◆§ A National Hallmark

The Talmud regards the natural restraint and modesty of the Jew as one of his most outstanding characteristics:

> Three fine qualities distinguish this nation of Israel: The Jews are compassionate, bashful, and performers of kindness (*Yevamos* 79a).

> Whoever displays these three traits is surely a descendant of Abraham, our father (*Kallah Rabbosi* #9).

When he fails to live up to the characteristics which define his spiritual identity, the Jew loses his national home:

> Jerusalem was destroyed only because its inhabitants had no shame or bashfulness before one another (*Shabbos* 119b).

◆§ The Ceaseless Breath of Life

כִּי לֹא עַל הַלֶּחֶם לְבַדּוֹ יִחְיֶה הָאָדָם כִּי עַל כָּל מוֹצָא פִי ה׳ יִחְיֶה הָאָדָם, *For not only by bread does man live, rather by all that emanates from the mouth of* HASHEM *does man enjoy life* (*Deuteronomy* 8:3)

Indeed, God perpetually vitalizes man's physical and spiritual being. Thus, *Reishis Chachmah* (*Shaar Ha'ahavah*, ch. 9) teaches one who takes his life for granted will not easily succeed in serving his Creator. The years of one's life are not a bequest, guaranteed for an extended period of time. Rather, each and ever breath of life is a new gift from

God: Man must be constantly thankful for the miracle of his existence. When one truly comprehends the extent of his dependency upon the Divine, he cannot help but lead a life of modest restraint.

⋙ Turning Inwards: Passion's Bridle

Rabbi Yehudah ben Teima said ... "The brazen person (*az panim*) heads towards the purgatory of Gehinnom, whereas the one who can be shame faced (*bosh panim*) is destined to enjoy the paradise of Gan Eden" *Avos* (5:23).

So powerful are the passions in man's heart that only a sense of God's Presence can help man to control them. At Sinai, the Almighty made His Presence vividly known to the Jewish people. Thus, when he weakens, the Jew must turn inwards and attune himself once again to the nearness of his Creator. As he does so, his feelings of shame become his most intense merit: "Whoever commits a transgression and is then ashamed of it, will be forgiven for all his sins" (*Berachos* 12b).

⋙ A Delicate Equilibrium

"Act with restraint in the company of others ..."

As the *Rambam* writes (*Shemoneh Perakim*, ch. 4), all character traits, even the most laudable, must be balanced. Although bashfulness and shame can be positive elements of character, they must not be felt excessively. The Mishnah teaches in *Avos* (2:6), לֹא הַבַּיְשָׁן לָמֵד, *The student who is excessively bashful will never learn anything*. Indeed, many situations call for an assertive response. As in much of life, the Jew must strive to achieve a delicate equilibrium.

24

וֶהֱוֵי זָהִיר לִקְרוֹת בַּתּוֹרָה תָּמִיד אֲשֶׁר תּוּכַל לְקַיְּמָהּ,
וְכַאֲשֶׁר תָּקוּם מִן הַסֵּפֶר, תְּחַפֵּשׂ בַּאֲשֶׁר לָמַדְתָּ
אִם יֵשׁ בּוֹ דָּבָר אֲשֶׁר תּוּכַל לְקַיְּמוֹ.

**Take care to always study Torah diligently
so that you will be able to fulfill its commands. When you rise from study, ponder
carefully what you have learned; see what
there is in it which you can put into practice.**

◆§ A Universal Obligation

Ramban here stresses that without diligent Torah study, it is
impossible to live properly as a Jew.
Rambam rules (*Hilchos Talmud Torah* 1:8-10):

> Every man is obligated to study Torah without exception —
> it makes no difference whether he is rich or poor, healthy or ill,
> young or old. Even the pauper who lives from alms and begs
> from door to door must study Torah. Even the man who is
> pressured to support a wife and children — every Jew must set
> aside definite times to study by day and by night ... one must
> continue to study until the day of his death.

Rambam also teaches (ibid. 3:12-13) that no matter what one's
intellectual capabilities, one can only truly succeed in his study if he fully
exerts himself:

> The Rabbis taught that the Torah can only be fully
> comprehended by those who "kill themselves" over it ... One

must take pain not to interrupt Torah study with frivolous conversation ... Our Sages taught (*Avos* 4:11): "Whoever neglects Torah study because of wealth will ultimately be forced to neglect it out of poverty. But whoever studies Torah despite poverty will ultimately fulfill it in wealth."

Rabbeinu Yonah (*Shaarei Teshuvah* III:14) writes that the *mitzvah* of Torah study is central; likewise, it carries with it heightened stakes: Just as the punishment for neglecting Torah study is harsh, so too is its reward greater than that of all other *mitzvos*.

◆§ Torah — An Instrument of Self-Knowledge

The Talmud (*Berachos* 5a) teaches:

If a person is beset by misfortune he should scrutinize his ways, as it is written: נַחְפְּשָׂה דְרָכֵינוּ וְנַחְקְרָה וְנָשׁוּבָה עַד ה', *Let us search and examine our ways and return to HASHEM* (*Lamentations* 3:40). If he fails to find his fault, then he may be assured that he has been punished for wasting time from Torah study.

The commentaries explain: No man is free from sin. If one intensively searched his soul and could find no wrongdoing, it can only be that he was equipped with inadequate tools in his search. More than anything else, Torah knowledge is this tool: It defines the extent of one's obligation to his Creator. If a man imagines himself to be spiritually flawless, he can thus be certain that he has not properly fulfilled his obligation of Torah study.

The Talmud (*Avodah Zarah* 20b) records that Rabbi Pinchas ben Yair formulated a detailed program for attaining perfect spiritual character. מִכָּאן אָמַר רַבִּי פִּנְחָס בֶּן יָאִיר: תּוֹרָה מְבִיאָה לִידֵי זְהִירוּת, זְהִירוּת מְבִיאָה לִידֵי זְרִיזוּת, *Rabbi Pinchas ben Yair said: "Torah leads to introspection; introspection leads to swift action."* If a person is not steeped in Torah he lacks a yardstick with which to measure himself. Torah study is thus a pre-requisite to effective introspection.

◆§ Greater than the Writing of Angels

The *Chofetz Chaim* attested that he learned to appreciate the value of Torah from Rav Yisrael Salanter. He once spent a night in a Vilna hotel sleeping in a room adjoining one occupied by Rav Yisrael. Late at night, he put his ear to the wall, and was awed by the sound of Rav Yisrael learning and repeating the *mishnah* in *Avos* (1:13): "He who fails to study Torah forfeits his right to life." The frightful but hushed tones he heard that night left an indelible impression upon him.

The *Chofetz Chaim* writes: "If we were told that archaeologists had just discovered a book written by the angel Gabriel, how we would yearn to read it. Yet here we have before us a book written by God Himself, and we overlook it!"

The *Chofetz Chaim* would also say: "Words of Torah are like precious gems; idle words are like dirt: One who interrupts his Torah study to engage in idle chatter is like the king who mixes dirt into the diamonds of his treasury."

~§ Keys of Diligence

The *Chazon Ish* (Collected Letters 1:3) writes:

> One whose study meets with constant interruption cannot hope to succeed: It is wise to devise ways to attain diligence. One possibility is to study a variety of subjects every day, so that each of them remain fresh; for example: Chumash with *Rashi*, mishnah, *mussar* and Talmud. It is also worthwhile to learn inside of a *beis hamidrash* and with a competent companion. But the most important thing to remember is that even when you study by yourself, you do so in the presence of *Hashem*. Never forget this!

~§ Captains of a Cosmic Voyage

Rabbi Elchonon Wasserman was once asked: "Why must the Jews study Torah ceaselessly and practice *mitzvos* constantly, while gentiles need keep only seven Noachide laws?" He answered with the following illustration:

The world can be compared to a luxury ocean liner. The moment the passengers come on board the crew hovers over them and offers them comforts and amenities. As the steward accompanies the guests to their staterooms, he makes one minor request: "Please take just a few moments to read this card which outlines the ship's general rules and emergency procedures. Then relax and have a carefree voyage."

At the same time, the captain boards the ship, lugging a heavy briefcase bulging with maps, charts, and navigational equipment. Unceremoniously, the captain stations himself at the helm of the ship. He holds firm to the steering system with a grip that never loosens. Ever alert, the captain's eyes study the maps, and gaze out to sea to spot danger. Through stressful days and sleepless nights the captain's vigil continues. Finally, he brings his ship safely into port.

Thus, during the voyage the passengers are pampered while the captain is pressured. But when they arrive at their destination the passengers merely depart, whereas the captain receives praise, reward and recognition.

Similarly, explained Rav Elchonon, the earth is a ship journeying through the sea of history. The nations of the world are passengers — while the people of Israel are captains. Thus, the Jews must diligently study the sea chart, their Torah, and use the navigational instruments, their *mitzvos*. Only then can they steer the world on a course towards it final Messianic destination. Only then, when the journey ends, will Israel, the captain of the ship, receive her appropriate recognition and reward.

25

וְתִפַּשְׁפֵּשׁ בְּמַעֲשֶׂיךָ בַּבֹּקֶר וּבָעֶרֶב.

Review your actions
every morning and evening.

๙ᕲ Introspection: A Constant Effort

Mesillas Yesharim (ch. 3) extols the virtues of *introspection* and encourages monitoring one's actions frequently:

> I see a need for a person to carefully examine his ways on a daily basis, just as successful merchants constantly supervise and evaluate their investments. One should designate a special time each day for his "personal accounting," to assure that it is conducted with undeviating regularity. Indeed, it yields valuable returns.

Mesillas Yesharim describes a two-pronged method of analysis. Quoting the Talmud in *Eruvin* 13b, he writes:

> יְפַשְׁפֵּשׁ בְּמַעֲשָׂיו — יְמַשְׁמֵשׁ בְּמַעֲשָׂיו, *One should scrutinize and evaluate his deeds. Scrutiny* here refers to the negative: one should first of all investigate his actions to see whether they harbor hidden wrongdoings or imperfections. Anything contrary to God's will he must strive to eradicate. Upon completion of *scrutiny*, one can begin the second phase, *evaluation.* Here, he inspects the good deeds that he performs. In this area, men are especially prey to self-deception, for it is difficult to admit to oneself the traces of negative motivations laced within his positive actions. If one honestly *evaluates* his positive deeds he is likely to discover pride, power, selfishness or personal satisfaction. When one subjects his actions to exhaustive investigation he is able to polish them to perfection.

ᐅᔥ The Prudent Customer

Vilna Gaon writes that פְּשְׁפּוּשׁ, *scrutiny*, and מִשְׁמוּשׁ, *examination*, lie at the very essence of the human experience. He quotes King Solomon in Proverbs: רַע רַע יֹאמַר הַקּוֹנֶה וְאֹזֵל לוֹ אָז יִתְהַלָּל, *"It is bad, it is bad!" says the buyer; but when he goes on his way, then he boasts* (Proverbs 20:14).

The prudent customer is demanding — he takes his time to check his purchase carefully before finally deciding upon it. The discriminating buyer sometimes rejects the first items which a salesperson shows him, protesting, as it were, "It is bad, it is bad!" The seller is thus forced to show him the very best merchandise he has to offer. Only after the deal is closed and the buyer is on his way does he finally say to himself, "The article I have bought is the very best!"

Similarly, says the *Vilna Gaon*, a person is placed on earth to acquire Torah, *mitzvos* and fine character traits. In his quest for these goals, one ought never be satisfied with what he has. As he strives to improve himself, he scrutinizes his earlier performance, saying, "It is bad, it is bad!" If he continues to demand of himself the highest standards, he will finish his life with a treasury of spiritual wealth.

ᐅᔥ Self-Examination: R' Yonah's Agenda

Rabbeinu Yonah of Gerondi, in his essay *Darkei HaTeshuvah* (printed in the *mussar* anthology, *Cheshbono Shel Olam*), maps out a detailed agenda for daily self-examination:

> From the moment a person awakens in the morning he should examine everything he does. One should divide his daily schedule into manageable segments which are easy to monitor. Let him say to himself: "I will keep myself under strict control until the first meal, breakfast; that's not too far off, I can surely do this." When he sits down to breakfast let him take stock of all that has transpired since he awoke. If he indeed erred, let him confess his mistake verbally, and resolve to be strong until lunch, when he re-examines his ways again. He then plans a method of self-control until his third meal when he makes a final accounting . . .

> The *Raavad* writes that mealtime is an appropriate setting for penitence and self-discipline. It is not necessary for the remorseful soul to afflict himself with debilitating fasts. Rather, one should seat himself down to a fine meal. While his appetite

is still keen, he may incorporate penance into his meals by refraining from eating the remainder of his food in order to honor his Maker. As he does so, he should think: "Just as I didn't give in to this desire, so will I not give in to any desire which is contrary to the will of my Maker." This type of abstinence will more effectively remind a person of his love for God than fasting for even a full day every week.

⋲§ The Flickering Candle

All his life Rav Yisrael Salanter subjected his thoughts and actions to intense scrutiny to find their flaws. It is told that he learned the importance of incessant toil for improvement from the following incident:

Late one night Rav Yisrael chanced to enter a shoemaker's home. The shoemaker was working by the light of a candle that flickered and threatened to go out at any moment. "Why are you still working?" asked Rav Yisrael, "The hour is late. Besides, your candle will soon be extinguished."

"This is true," answered the shoemaker, "yet as long as the candle still burns, it is possible to work and to repair."

Rav Yisrael was deeply impressed by these words. He pondered the shoemaker's dedication, and reflected: If one must work so for his physical needs, how much more must he never cease his spiritual growth so long as his soul flickers within him. For days after, Rav Yisrael was heard pacing his room, sometimes chanting slowly, "As long as the candle is burning, it is still possible to work and to repair."

Once while Rav Yisrael was sitting with his students, a dignitary of the city came to ask a question. At the beginning of the conversation Rav Yisrael sighed deeply. The conversation continued, and soon the dignitary left. Afterwards, the students asked what had caused him to sigh. "The moment this respected man came before me," he replied, "I noticed that the hem of my garment was torn and I felt embarrassed. Then I said to myself, 'If I was embarrassed before a human being because of a slight tear in my clothes, imagine how great and bitter a person's shame is in the World to Come if the flaws in his soul are not repaired while there is yet time.' "

26

וּבָזֶה יִהְיוּ כָּל יָמֶיךָ בִּתְשׁוּבָה.

And in this way live all your days in repentance.

Ramban's words derive from the Talmud (*Shabbos* 153a): Rabbi Eliezer said: שׁוּב יוֹם אֶחָד לִפְנֵי מִיתָתְךָ, *Repent one day before your death.*

His disciples asked him, "Does a man then know on what day he will die?"

"All the more reason that he repent today," he replied, "for perhaps he shall die tomorrow. Thus, his whole life shall be one of repentance."

⊷§ *Ceaseless Renewal*

The Hebrew word for repentance is תְּשׁוּבָה, literally, *return*. When man searches his actions and refines them he draws closer to his Creator. This process of spiritual renewal, as the *Ramban* writes, is at its best when it is perpetual. Although Jews strive to become especially attuned to the presence of their Maker during the month of *Elul* and the Ten Days of Penitence, in truth, there is no "season" for repentance.

Rav Yisrael Salanter used to say: "Generally people work on repentance during the Ten Days of Penitence from Rosh Hashanah to Yom Kippur. The more pious ones begins to work on repentance from the beginning of the month of Elul. But I say that repentance must begin right after *Ne'ilah*."

Rav Yisrael was indeed a model for this. If he sometimes failed to concentrate sufficiently during prayers, he would devise strategies for correcting his failure. He would maintain a personal record of even the most minor actions. For fifteen years he was regretful for having once forgotten to check for *chametz* before Pesach in the bin where he stored his salt.

◆§ The Unknown Path

Rabbeinu Yonah of Gerondi wrote a classic text on the subject of repentance entitled: *Shaarei Teshuvah*, "The Gates of Repentance." He begins his work quoting a parable of the man who neglects to seize the opportunity of *teshuvah:*

> In the Midrash (*Kohelles Rabbah* 7:15) our Sages, of blessed memory, compared his situation to that of a band of thieves. Having been captured and imprisoned by the king, together they dug a tunnel through which to escape the dungeon. All escaped but one gang member, who was afraid of the unknown path which lay before him. When the jail warden discovered the breach and saw the man who stayed behind, he began to strike him with his rod, exclaiming: "Miserable soul! Don't you see the breach opened wide before you — why did you not seize the opportunity to save yourself as well?" (*Shaarei Teshuvah* I:2).

◆§ Rambam's Rebuke

A man who considered himself pious once announced to *Rambam* (Maimonides) that he saw no reason to recite the traditional confession of sins on Yom Kippur, for he was innocent of all of them. Moreover, explained the man, "If I were to confess these sins it would simply be a lie; how does one dare to lie in the face of God?" *Chida* in *Midbar Kedeimos* (6:11) records *Rambam's* response:

> My dear man, your words betray that you simply have little concept of what it means to serve the Almighty. Our duties toward God are unlimited: They are complex, and no man in the world can finally fulfill them ... If your self-appraisal would be objective, you would discover that every day of your life you in some way transgress every sin listed in the *viduy* confession of Yom Kippur.
>
> Furthermore, bear in mind that the greater a man is, the more grievous are his minor mis-steps. King David was involved with Bath Sheba — no longer a married woman because her husband, Uriah, had divorced her. Nevertheless, because David was an exceptionally pious man, the indiscretion he committed — while negligible for a lesser person — was considered tantamount to adultery for him.

Rav Saadyah Gaon taught his disciples to examine their ways every day even if they felt certain that they had not sinned. Rav Saadyah himself adopted this practice after the following incident:

Once, Rav Saadyah lodged with an innkeeper who was ignorant of his illustrious guest's true identity. He put the Rav in a simple room and served him as he would his regular guests. When word escaped that the leader of the generation was passing through the town, all the townsfolk flocked to the inn to glimpse Rav Saadyah. The innkeeper finally realized who his illustrious guest was, and approached the Rav, with tears streaming down his cheeks.

"Rebbi, please forgive me!"

"Forgive you? What have you done wrong? You treated me very well," came the response.

"Rebbi! I didn't know who you were! Believe me, had I known that the great Rav Saadyah Gaon was staying under my roof I would have treated you like royalty!"

Upon hearing these sincere words, Rav Saadyah himself burst into tears. He explained, "From your words I perceived for myself the extent of our obligation towards our King, *Hashem.* Previously, I felt I served *Hashem* well, but now I realize that I am lacking. For just as your service of me changes as you more clearly perceive my identity, so it is with my service of God. With each passing day I discover new levels of God's kindness towards me: I realize that whatever respect and service I offered God yesterday was woefully insufficient, for had I known *then* what I know about God *now*, I would have served Him with even greater devotion and intensity. Life is indeed a constant cycle of rediscovery in which man sheds the relative ignorance of the past!"

27

וְהָסֵר כָּל דִּבְרֵי הָעוֹלָם מִלִּבְּךָ בְּעֵת הַתְּפִלָּה,
וְהָכֵן לִבְּךָ לִפְנֵי הַמָּקוֹם ב״ה.

Cast external matters from your mind when you stand to pray; carefully prepare your heart in the presence of the Holy One.

Ramban's concept is codified by the *Rama* in *Shulchan Aruch* (*Orach Chaim* 98:1):

> Before one begins to pray, let him meditate upon the loftiness of God and the lowliness of man; let him pluck from his heart his yearning for the mundane pleasures of the world.
>
> It is prohibited even for a father to kiss his children in the synagogue — he must establish in his heart that there is no love comparable to his love of the Almighty God.

Request: The Nature of Prayer

A question arises: How can the *Ramban* encourage his son to "cast worldly matters from your mind when you stand to pray" when the very nature of prayer is a request of God to grant us the blessings of this world — health, prosperity, freedom and success?

We find an answer in the carefully chosen words of *Rama* quoted above: "In prayer ... let him pluck from his heart his yearning for *the mundane pleasures* of this world" — certainly we pray for the bounty of this world, but we strive to elevate our requests above the mundane. We ask God to make the resources of this world available to us so we can utilize them as tools to serve Him properly and in peace of mind.

Rabbi Chaim of Volozhin (*Nefesh HaChaim, Shaar* II) demonstrates that the true purpose of prayer is to increase God's sovereignty over the world: We ask for blessings from His hand so that God's influence should permeate the world with greater intensity. In genuine prayer, the supplicant learns how to use this world as a springboard to propel himself heavenward to new spiritual heights.

⋙ "We Are Your Creations"

Ramban himself, in his commentary to the Torah (*Exodus* 13:12), offers a soul-stirring description of the purpose of prayer:

> The intent of all commandments is that we acquire a firm belief in God, and proclaim Him as the One who has created us. This is, in fact, the very purpose of creation — for there is no other motive known to us. The Supreme Being asks of man only that he come to know Him and testify that He is the Creator. The prayers we recite, the synagogues we build, the convocations we hold — all are designed to give outward expression to our inner conviction that He is our Creator. We assemble in the House of Prayer and cry out: בְּרִיּוֹתֶךָ אֲנַחְנוּ, *We are Your creations!*

⋙ Kavanah — Direction in Prayer

The Talmud (*Berachos* 31a) teaches that, "He who prays must direct his heart to heaven." Prayer is the pathway to God. When following a path, *kavanah* — direction — is everything. תְּפִלָּה בְּלִי כַּוָּנָה כְּגוּף בְּלִי נְשָׁמָה, *Prayer without proper intention and direction is like a body without a soul.*

The essence of direction is to know one's destination:

> When Rabbi Eliezer was on his sickbed his disciples came to visit him and asked, "Our master, teach us the pathways of life so that we may reach the World to Come!"
>
> Rabbi Eliezer said, "... When you stand in prayer, know before Whom you are praying — thus will you merit the World to Come." (*Berachos* 28b).

⋙ The Moment of Prayer: Man Is Not Alone

Prayer is a moment of transformation. Before he speaks to God, man is alone and frightened; weak and torn by worries which threaten to overwhelm him. When the moment of prayer arrives, man understands that he has a caring and sympathetic ear to talk to. He turns to his loving Father in Heaven and admits frailty: He allows the weighty burdens to slip off his shoulders in the realization that he is not alone. *Cast upon HASHEM your burden, and He will sustain you, He will never allow the righteous to falter (Psalms 55:23).*

HaRav Yechezkel Levenstein writes in his work on *Emunah* (pp. 182-183) that one should stand in prayer like a beggar standing at the door with outstretched palms. The supplicant must fill himself with the awareness that his existence is entirely dependent upon God. When one elevates himself to this level of humility, then his life's sustenance becomes truly independent of the hand of man, and a direct gift of the Almighty.

~§ Technology: The Illusion of Power

As man has strengthened his technological hold on the world, nature has finally lost some of the stranglehold on his life. We can predict the weather with confidence (if only for the weekend). We have lights to wash away the night, central air-conditioning to make the sun outside go away, and airplanes with which to escape the harshness of winter. We seem to have reached the pinnacles of technological success — are we yet sovereigns of our destiny?

Man shall never really conquer nature: Pitted against the backdrop of the starry cosmos, he still trembles at the grandeur of his Creator. Nonetheless, on a daily level, modern man finds it difficult to sense his helplessness. Ultimately this can be his greatest stumbling block in the pathway to genuine, meaningful prayer. In overcoming this block one must learn well the *Ramban's* previous lessons in humility, before he can properly approach prayer.

~§ Altering Destiny: Altering Oneself

Rabbi Yoseph Albo (*Sefer HaIkkarim*, IV:18) asks: "How does a mortal dare to approach the Almighty in prayer to ask Him to change His decrees? God certainly knows what is best for man! How can we have the audacity to request a change of the Divine design of events?" He answers that one who prays properly undergoes a literal process of transformation. Thus, אִם תִּשְׁתַּנֶּה הַהֲכָנָה תִּשְׁתַּנֶּה הַגְּזֵרָה, "When one's character changes, then the Divine decree against him changes accordingly."

◄§ The Shell and the Kernel

Chovos Halevavos (Shaar Cheshbon Hanefesh, Ch. III, section 9) gives detailed instructions on how to prepare for prayer:

> One must disengage himself from this world and free his mind of any thought which will distract his attention from prayer. One should seriously take to heart that he stands before his Maker, and should carefully choose both the words and the themes he intends to contemplate.
>
> Understand this well — the words of prayer enunciated by the mouth are merely the shell. The heart's meditation upon these words is the inner kernel. Words are like the body of prayer, while meditation is the soul. One who prays only with his tongue, while his mind wanders, resembles an empty body, a husk devoid of a kernel.
>
> Such a person is compared to the servant whose master had just returned home from a journey. The servant sent his children to greet the master, while he himself ignored the master's presence. The master was infuriated by this wanton disrespect. Similarly, if the heart sends the body and the mouth to greet the Almighty in prayer, if the heart itself turns its attention elsewhere, God will surely be displeased.

He concludes:

> My dear brother, it is only proper that you realize what prayer really is! It is nothing less than the passionate yearning of the soul for God, and its utter surrender before Him.

28

וְתֶחֱשֹׁב הַדִּבּוּר קֹדֶם שֶׁתּוֹצִיאֶנּוּ מִפִּיךָ . . . וּתְפִלָּתְךָ
תִּהְיֶה זַכָּה וּבָרָה וּנְקִיָּה וּמְכֻוֶּנֶת וּמְקֻבֶּלֶת לִפְנֵי
הַמָּקוֹם ב"ה, שֶׁנֶּאֱמַר: תָּכִין לִבָּם תַּקְשִׁיב אָזְנֶךָ.

**Ponder your words before you utter them
. . . Your prayer will be pure and clear,
sincere and pleasing to God, Blessed is He,
as it is written: You prepare their heart
[to concentrate], You are attentive
[to their prayers] *(Psalms 10:17).***

Ramban exhorts his son to make his prayer זַכָּה, *pure*. In this, he alludes to the words of the Midrash (*Shemos Rabbah* 22:4) which states:

> Job said of himself, עַל לֹא חָמָס בְּכַפָּי וּתְפִלָּתִי זַכָּה, *No injustice is in my hands and my prayer is pure* (Job 16:17). This implies that both a pure prayer and sullied prayer exist. The man whose hands are filthied by dishonest gain cries out, yet the Almighty turns away from his prayers; for his plea is tainted. But Job's prayer was זַכָּה, *pure*. He was honest, and his hands were thus clean.

◆§ The Obligation of Prayer: A Dispute

There is a halachic dispute regarding the nature of the obligation to pray daily. *Rambam's* opinion in *Sefer HaMitzvos* (*Mitzvah #5*) is that there is a Biblical commandment to pray to God every day, as it is written: וַעֲבַדְתֶּם אֵת ה' אֱלֹהֵיכֶם, *And you should serve HASHEM your God* (*Exodus* 23:25), . . . true service of God is through prayer.

Ramban in his commentary (ibid.) disagrees, and maintains that prayer, by its very nature, cannot be a Scriptural obligation, for it is a spontaneous outpouring of the heart. Prayer is, rather, a wonderful gift: God, in His kindness, allows the Jewish people to cry out whenever they need Him, and to rest assured that He will respond to their sincere supplication.

⁓§ Prayer: A Cosmic Force

Tur Shulchan Aruch (*Orach Chaim* #113) writes of *Chassidei Ashkenaz* — the pious mystics of medieval Germany — who meticulously studied the significance of each word in the *Shemoneh Esrei*. These scholars demonstrated how no word is superfluous and derived insights from even the number of words in each benediction.

Rabbi Chaim of Volozhin (*Nefesh HaChaim* II:13) writes of the importance of every word of the *Amidah* prayer:

> The *Anshei Knesses HaGedolah*, the Men of the Great Assembly who composed the text of the *Amidah*, numbered one hundred and twenty scholars. Some of these were more than Sages — they were prophets as well. What these men achieved can never be duplicated. They invested each word of the liturgy with a power to affect all of creation, from the smallest atomic particle to the most enormous galactic mass.

> Moreover, the effect of every word never remains the same. Each time a person prays his words leave a different impression on the cosmos. The impact of the evening prayer is not the same as the impact of the prayer offered on the previous morning. Ponder this: The Men of the Great Assembly composed their words of prayer thousands of years ago — from that time until the advent of the Messiah, myriads upon myriads of prayers will be uttered — and no two prayers are alike. All this is possible because a spirit of Divine prophecy guided the authors: Through them the Almighty Himself implanted within each word infinite power and unlimited effect.

> Since no human being can possibly fathom the awesome depth of each word of prayer, one should rather pray with pure and simple intent. As he pronounces each word, he should picture in his mind's eye a mental image of the actual word as it

is written. He should concentrate on raising the words heavenward to their celestial source ... One who prays in this fashion will truly make an impact with every word he utters.

✑ Concentrate on Every Word

The Talmud (*Berachos* 30b) describes how the *Chassidim HaRishonim* — the pious men of earlier generations — would meditate for a full hour *before* they recited the *Amidah* (*Shemoneh Esrei*) and then would actually spend one complete hour (sixty minutes; 3600 seconds) reciting their prayers. Since there are approximately 500 words in *Shemoneh Esrei*, this would allot an average of seven seconds for each word. This demonstrates how slowly and deliberately one must concentrate on each and every word.

✑ A Crown of Prayers

Arvei Nachal (*Vayakhel*) writes that God wears a glorious wreath woven of the prayers of Israel. Each word of prayer, uttered with pure intent, is a precious gem which Hashem uses to adorn this crown. He continues: God scattered and concealed holy sparks all over the world. Whenever a person prays with intent, his words attract one of these lost sparks and propels it heavenward to add brilliance and sparkle to God's glorious crown.

Arvei Nachal (*Vaeschanan*) writes as well of another ramification of prayer: It serves as the key to a heavenly vault of blessing. With proper concentration and pure intent the words of prayer unlock each treasury, causing their bounty to overflow — not just for the benefit of the supplicant but for the good of the entire world.

✑ The Gift of Ecstasy

Rabbi Levi Yitzchak of Berditchev (*Kedushas Levi, Mishpatim*) writes that every Jew must strive to delight his Maker. This is the ultimate goal of observance. When God "delights" in his prayer, man senses his success: He feels his heart suffused with fire and passion for all that is sacred — ardor and ecstasy are Divine gifts which God bestows upon beloved servants.

Sefer Chassidim (#18) teaches that prayer and joy are natural companions:

הִתְהַלְלוּ בְּשֵׁם קָדְשׁוֹ יִשְׂמַח לֵב מְבַקְשֵׁי ה׳, *Glory in His Holy Name; be glad of heart, you who seek* HASHEM (*I Chronicles* 16:10). David, king of Israel, accompanied his prayers and praise with music of his lyre, in order to fill his heart with ecstasy and love for God.

Elsewhere, *Sefer Chassidim* (#773) writes:

If one prays and suddenly his heart is filled with a surge of joy and love for God, he should understand that God has chosen to fulfill his wishes, as it says: וְהִתְעַנַּג עַל ה׳ וְיִתֶּן לְךָ מִשְׁאֲלֹת לִבֶּךָ, *And find delight in* HASHEM, *and He will grant you the desires of your heart* (*Psalms* 37:4). If this Divine ecstasy should come during the *Shemoneh Esrei* service, especially in the blessing of *Shema Koleinu*, "Hear our voices," then he should conclude his prayers with the following personal supplication: "May it be Your will, O God, that this ecstatic love be forever bound to my heart and firmly implanted therein. Let my children experience this love as well."

If one experiences a surge of ecstasy at any time of day or night — not during prayers — he should cherish this precious moment and remain silent as the intensity of his feelings subsides. These wonderful moments of passionate Divine love are similar to the revelations of the prophets of old. The experience is other-worldly.

29

תִּקְרָא הָאִגֶּרֶת הַזֹּאת פַּעַם אַחַת בַּשָּׁבוּעַ וְלֹא
תִפְחוֹת, לְקַיְּמָהּ וְלָלֶכֶת בָּהּ תָּמִיד
אַחַר הַשֵּׁם יִתְבָּרַךְ.

**Read this letter once a week and neglect
none of it. Fulfill it, and in so doing, walk
with it forever in the ways of Hashem, may
He be Blessed.**

◦§ In God's Footsteps

The Torah commands וְהָלַכְתָּ בִּדְרָכָיו, *And you shall follow in His
[God's] ways* (*Deuteronomy* 28:9). Simply, this means that one ought
emulate the attributes of the Almighty described in the Torah. Just as
God is compassionate, merciful and holy, so must the Jew strive to be
compassionate, merciful and holy (see *Rambam, Hilchos De'os* 1:5).
Ramban here alludes to a different level of walking in God's ways —
one discussed by *Rambam* in his *Guide* (III:51):

One who walks with God, writes *Rambam*, rivets his attention to the
Almighty and allows nothing to distract him. It is this "walking in the
way of God" which is the highest level of human existence: It can only
be attained after intense discipline. One who aspires to such closeness to
his Maker, he writes, should begin by training himself to concentrate on
his prayers. After training himself in this, he will have the ability to
more easily sense God's presence throughout the day, even when
involved in mundane pursuits.

Rambam continues:

When a man frees his thoughts from all worldly matters — when he obtains a correct understanding of the true nature of God and rejoices in that knowledge — it is impossible for any kind of evil to befall him. He is always with God and God is always with him.

◄§"There is Nothing Besides Him"

Rabbi Chaim of Volozhin (*Nefesh HaChaim* III:12-13) cites the Talmud (*Chullin* 7b), which teaches that if a person internalizes the verse: ה׳ הוּא הָאֱלֹהִים אֵין עוֹד מִלְבַדּוֹ, *HASHEM, He is God, there is nothing else beside Him* (*Deuteronomy* 4:35), he will be protected from harmful forces. When one accepts God's absolute sovereignty he places himself fully under His protective wing. Although nature contains many destructive elements, the man of faith understands that they are but marionettes in the hands of the Creator.

◄§ Nature's Leash

The Brisker Rav, Rav Yitzchak Zev Soloveitchik, was a descendant of Rav Chaim of Volozhin — the author of *Nefesh HaChaim*. He testified how the statement of faith recorded in *Nefesh HaChaim* literally served as a guide through his life. When he was a young man, "Reb Velvel" — as the Brisker Rav was fondly known — was commanded to appear before the Russian draft board to be inducted into the Czar's army. This fate was tantamount to both a spiritual and physical death sentence. As the date of his appearance neared, his father, Rav Chaim Brisker, instructed him to concentrate on the above passage from *Nefesh HaChaim*. To R' Velvel's great relief, his meeting with the draft board came, and he was exempted from the draft.

Later, when the Germans occupied Poland at the beginning of World War II, Reb Velvel fled from Warsaw to Vilna. The roads were filled with German troops, and Nazis were everywhere. The danger was awesome. Yet, Reb Velvel traveled along undaunted, for he never stopped reviewing the pledge of the *Nefesh HaChaim*: "If you always think of God, He will always think of you, and protect you from all harm."

Just once, Reb Velvel was distracted and his mind wandered onto another thought. Immediately, as if from nowhere, an armed Nazi approached him threateningly. In a flash, Reb Velvel collected his thoughts and focused on the *Nefesh HaChaim* and the Nazi moved on (*Rabboseinu* p. 170).

Rabbi Yosef Leib Bloch of Telshe (*Shiurei Daas*, II:44) explains that natural forces which threaten mankind can be compared to a vicious dog with a long leash tied to its neck. When the animal pounces, the only way an intended victim can save himself is by calling to the dog's master, to restrain the beast. If the victim fails to recognize the presence of the master then he is truly in grave danger. Similarly when man fails to perceive the "leash" upon the forces of nature, he indeed places himself at their mercy.

30

לְמַעַן תַּצְלִיחַ בְּכָל דְּרָכֶיךָ
וְתִזְכֶּה לְעוֹלָם הַבָּא הַצָּפוּן לַצַּדִּיקִים.

So that you may succeed in your ways
and merit the World to Come
that lies hidden for the righteous.

◄§ A Time for Work — a Time for Respite

As *Ramban* concludes his letter, he reveals the inner workings of the righteous man's mind. What mental attitude should one adopt in order to achieve piety and humility? Writes the *Ramban:* A person must simply say to himself: "I will reserve my enjoyment for the World to Come."

This world is not conducive to real pleasure . . . it is too fleeting. It is a life of change, a life of work. Sabbath, a glimpse of the World to Come, is our only true respite. As the Talmud (*Eruvin* 22a) teaches: הַיּוֹם לַעֲשׂוֹתָם וּמָחָר לְקַבֵּל שְׂכָרָם, "Today is the time for their [commandments] performance, tomorrow is the time for their payment." *Deferred payment* is the essential mental attitude of the righteous — *instant gratification*, they realize, is ultimately empty.

The Talmud (*Kiddushin* 39b) teaches that: שְׂכַר מִצְוָה בְּהַאי עַלְמָא לֵיכָּא, *The reward for mitzvos is not to be found in this world.* Vilna Gaon comments: דְּלֵיכָּא בְּמַאי לְאִשְׁתַּלּוּמֵי, *for nothing in this world is adequate enough to serve as fair payment.*

R' Yitzchak Zev Soloveitchik told the following about R' Aryeh Leib of Metz, author of the classic work "Shaagas Aryeh":

All through their lives, Rav Aryeh Leib and his pious wife lived in dire poverty. However, at the age of seventy, the *Shaagas Aryeh* assumed the position of Rav in the prosperous and prestigious *kehillah* of Metz. Soon after their arrival in Metz, the Rebbetzin hosted a dinner in honor of the community leaders. The *kehillah* was considerate enough to deliver the food for this event to their Rav's home. Included were delicacies which the Rebbetzin had never before seen. She was particularly puzzled by a bag of white granular crystals, which she assumed to be a special dish.

After the meal the Rebbetzin served the sweet crystals, which people told her was called sugar. After enjoying some of this delicious sugar the Rebbetzin approached the Rav and burst into tears: "Woe unto us!" she cried. "All of our lives we took no pleasure from this world so we could fully enjoy the World to Come. But look, now we have faltered, and have tasted of our portion in this world."

The Midrash (*Bamidbar Rabbah* 21:18) teaches how those who seek gratification in this world are condemned to lives of frustration and disappointment:

> Rabbi Dustai related: "I was once invited to a sumptuous banquet hosted by a prominent and prosperous idol worshiper who demanded that every single person in our city attend the enormous, lavish feast which he has prepared with unsurpassed grandeur. The elegant tables were laden with every possible food and delicacy in the world. The host was beaming with pride as he boasted that there was absolutely nothing missing from his banquet tables. All of a sudden someone discovered that a certain type of exotic nut was not to be found on the table. In an instant the host's facial expression was transformed. His features were twisted into contortions of fury and wrath. He ranted and he fumed. And then he grabbed the banquet table and overturned it and smashed everything to pieces. I asked the man why he was so angry and he replied: 'Rabbi, you always taught — and I believe you — that this world is for us idolaters to enjoy, whereas the World to Come is reserved for you Jews. Now I see that I cannot enjoy everything in this world, so I became angry.'"

Since *Ramban* is instructing his son in this letter on how to achieve peace of mind and tranquility, he found it necessary to emphasize that thought of reward should be reserved for the future, for to expect reward and gratification here in this world is sure to lead to frustration.

๑§ Observance and Reward

Ramban, in his commentary to the Torah (*Leviticus* 18:4), teaches that the intent of the heart is a prime consideration in the Divine reckoning of man's deeds. As men's motivation differ, so their rewards differ.

> Know that man's reward for observance of the commandments is in accordance with the intent of his heart. He who observes the commandments for the purpose of receiving reward will accordingly be blessed in this world with many years of life, much riches and glory. He who observes the commandments for the purpose of being rewarded in heaven will attain his desire as well ... his soul will come to rest in the World to Come. However, the person who observes with no thought of reward at all, only out of a sense of love of God, however, will attain blessings both in this world and in the Coming World.

Chovos Halevavos (*Shaar Habitachon*, ch. 4) writes:

> There are two types of good deeds. Some, like the duties of the heart, are concealed and known only to the Creator. Other good deeds entail physical action and are, therefore, apparent to all. For the fulfillment of good deeds which are visible, the Almighty bestows a reward which is visible in this world; but for the fulfillment of good deeds in secret, God reserves and hides away recompense for the World to Come.

๑§ The Heavenly Jewel

The Midrash (*Shemos Rabbah* 52:3) tells a story of Rabbi Shimon ben Chalafta, who was so poor that he once had nothing to eat for *Shabbos*. He went to a secluded area outside the city and poured his heart out before the Almighty, Who answered by presenting the Rabbi with a precious jewel. Rabbi Shimon sold the jewel and purchased his *Shabbos* needs. When the Rabbi brought all this home, his good wife inquired: "Where is all this from?"

"From the sustenance provided by God," replied the Rabbi.

His wife was adamant: "If you don't tell me exactly where this is from, I will not eat from it."

And so Rabbi Shimon told her the story of how God answered his prayers with a precious jewel from Heaven. The wife stood firm. "I will not taste a thing all *Shabbos* unless you promise to return the jewel after *Shabbos* is over."

"Why do you insist on this?' asked the puzzled husband.

She replied: "Don't you realize that this gem was removed from the table of delights which is prepared for you to enjoy in the Here-after? Do you really want your eternal table of reward to be partially empty?"

Rabbi Shimon considered these words and went to discuss the matter with his master, Rabbi Judah the prince. Rabbi Judah comforted his beloved disciple: "Tell your wife that she should not fear. If taking this gem will leave an empty gap in your eternal table, I promise to fill in the loss with the rewards amassed for me on my table." Rabbi Shimon related this to his wife but she still refused to partake. She came before Rabbi Judah the prince and asked: "Rabbi how can you propose to transfer reward from one table to another in the Hereafter? You know that in the World to Come one *tzaddik* cannot see another *tzaddik*, for each and every one dwells in a world of bliss entirely of his own." Rabbi Judah relented, and Rabbi Shimon returned the precious gem so as not to detract from his eternal reward.

⸢§ The Terrestrial Cave

Sefer HaYoshor (ch. 12) illustrates the incomprehensibility of the World to Come to mortals who dwell on this earth:

> This world may be likened to a cave buried deep in the ground, cut off from surface contact. The men who inhabit this subterranean vault know nothing beyond their walls and dark tunnels. Their concept of reality is based on their restricted environment.
>
> Imagine how utterly amazed and overwhelmed these cave-men would be if they emerged from their confinement to behold vast stretches of open land, soaring mountains and rolling seas — all of the countless wonders of nature. How they

would be dazzled by the brilliance of the sun and the stars and the endless heaven!

Humans confined to this earth are, thus, like cavemen who have no concept of reality. It is only when man dies that he emerges from his terrestrial cave and beholds the endless splendor of the Real World — the World to Come!

Epilogue

וּבְכָל יוֹם שֶׁתִּקְרָאֶנָּה יַעֲנוּךְ מִן הַשָּׁמַיִם כַּאֲשֶׁר
יַעֲלֶה עַל לִבְּךָ לִשְׁאוֹל עַד עוֹלָם אָמֵן סֶלָה.

**Every day that you shall read this letter,
heaven shall answer your heart's desires
. . . Amen, Selah!**

◄§ Answered Prayer

In his closing remarks, *Ramban* reveals the formula for effective, meaningful prayer. He states that after one reads his letter, "They will answer you according to your heart's desires." This alludes to the teaching: "Treat God's will as if it were your will, so that God will treat your will as if it were His will" (*Avos* 2:4).

One who faithfully follows the teachings of *Ramban's* letter will inevitably train his heart to desire only that which God desires. Therefore, God will surely treat this person's will as if it were His own.

This is *not* supernatural; for those who pray properly, it is quite natural.

◄§ The Extraordinary Is Natural

In *Psalms* (145:18) we read: קָרוֹב ה' לְכָל קֹרְאָיו לְכֹל אֲשֶׁר יִקְרָאֻהוּ בֶאֱמֶת, *HASHEM is close to all who call upon Him — to all who call upon Him sincerely.* The second half of the verse answers the obvious question raised by the first half: How can we claim that God is close to *all who call upon Him* when we see that so many prayers go unanswered? In

120 / A Letter for the Ages

reply, the Psalmist emphasizes that this guarantee of Divine closeness is limited to *all who call upon Him sincerely*, i.e., with total and unswerving confidence. When a person looks to other forces for salvation, he cannot be considered as one who *calls sincerely*. Even though, as a creature of this world, he must turn to doctors, bankers, or generals, he must do so with the awareness that they are but God's tools. The ultimate power is His.

The lessons of this letter prepare a person to pray sincerely, because humility and faith cause him to recognize that everything is in the hands of God, while man and his machines have no independent sway.

Maharsha (*Kiddushin* 29b) states emphatically that the Talmudic dictum, אֵין סוֹמְכִין עַל הַנֵּס, *We should not rely on a miracle* (*Pesachim* 64b), applies only if a person fails to pray. When a person prays sincerely, however, it is *natural* for even the most extraordinary things to happen.

Ramban himself supports this view in his commentary to *Deuteronomy* 34:10 where he observes that all the miracles performed by the prophets came as a result of their prayers. By virtue of sincere prayer, Joshua stopped the sun and Elijah and Elisha resurrected the dead. Thus, even the greatest prophets were not endowed with mysterious supernatural powers; rather, their prophetic spirit brought them closer to God so that they could pray with great intimacy and trust in the Almighty.

◆§ Every Prayer Is Answered

Even when a person prays sincerely, there is no assurance that God will give him exactly what he requests — only that heartfelt prayer is never in vain.

When Rav Shneur Kotler, *Rosh Yeshivah* of Beis Midrash Govoha of Lakewood, was suffering from his terminal illness, a group of his students and admirers journeyed to Bnei Brak, Israel, to implore the holy Steipler Gaon to intensify his prayers on his behalf. They confided to the Steipler that they were discouraged because prayers were pouring out of tens of thousands of Jewish hearts, yet the *Rosh Yeshivah's* condition continued to decline.

The Steipler responded: "Do not be dismayed. There is no such thing as a sincere prayer that goes unanswered. Any heartfelt request addressed to God *must* be answered. It can't be otherwise. If it is not answered today it will be answered tomorrow. If not tomorrow it will be answered in a week. If not a week, in a month. If not answered in a month it may be answered in a year, or in ten years, or in one hundred years or more. If your prayers are not answered in your lifetime they will be answered for your children or for your children's children. We cannot say for sure *when* a prayer will be answered, we can rest assured only that every prayer *will* be answered somehow, someday."

◄§ *In Ramban's Merit*

Finally, since *Ramban* assured people reading his Letter that their prayers would be answered, the supplicant should specifically include in his prayers a plea that his petition be fulfilled in the merit of *Ramban*.

This is based on the Talmud (*Bava Metziah* 84b) which relates how sixty sailors once came to give Rabbi Elazar ben Shimon a gift of sixty chests of treasure. *Rashi* explains that while at sea a huge storm-tossed wave threatened to capsize their ship. The sailors begged God to save them in the merit of the pious Rabbi Elazar ben Shimon. In the *tzaddik's* merit the sea was calmed. Now the sailors came with gifts to show him their appreciation.

Similarly, if one asks that his prayers be answered in the merit of *Ramban*, he may feel confident that his petition will be fulfilled.

◄§ *Ramban's Legacy*

In his ethical will, *Ramban* left a rich legacy both to his son, Nachman, and to generations upon generations of Jews who are his disciples and the heirs of his mind and spirit.

The essence of his message is that humility and self-control can enable a person to achieve tranquility and peace of mind. One who acquires these Godly traits will learn how to speak to God in sincere prayer. And when a Godly person speaks sincerely — God himself listens and answers the supplicant!

This volume is part of
THE ARTSCROLL SERIES®
an ongoing project of
translations, commentaries and expositions
on Scripture, Mishnah, liturgy, history,
the classic Rabbinic Writings,
biographies, and thought.

For a brochure of current publications
visit your local Hebrew bookseller
or contact the publisher:

Mesorah Publications, Ltd.

4401 Second Avenue
Brooklyn, New York 11232
(718) 921-9000